Child Abuse

A Study of Inquiry Reports
1973 – 1981

LONDON   HER MAJESTY'S STATIONERY OFFICE

ISBN 0 11 320788 3

HER MAJESTY'S STATIONERY OFFICE

Government Bookshops

49 High Holborn, London WC1V 6HB
13a Castle Street, Edinburgh EH2 3AR
Brazennose Street, Manchester M60 8AS
Southey House, Wine Street, Bristol BS1 2BQ
258 Broad Street, Birmingham B1 2HE
80 Chichester Street, Belfast BT1 4JY

*Government publications are also available
through booksellers*

"..........a story unfolds in the report of small carelessnesses, pressures of other work, difficulties of staffing and human procrastinations and failure to co-operate, by which few workers, if they are honest, have not at times been tempted from their standards, but which collectively resulted in individual tragedy and public scandal." Jean Heywood, writing in 1958 about the Monckton inquiry, which was set up in 1945 after the death of Dennis O'Neill whilst in care. (Jean Heywood: *Children in Care*. Routledge and Kegan Paul, 1959.)

Foreword

Over the last ten years there has been grave and continuing public concern about the problem of child abuse. Much has been done to detect, prevent and deal with it more effectively.

But we cannot afford to be complacent. The agencies concerned on the ground and the central Government Departments need to keep the problem constantly under review. As part of this process, DHSS staff have carried out this study which presents an analysis of the published reports of inquiries into eighteen cases of abuse, seventeen of which involved the death of a child.

The study does not contain official guidance, but it says much of interest and relevance to all the agencies concerned—social services, health services, education, police, probation, the courts and the voluntary sector.

I hope all of them will use the study to help make their work even more effective. Nothing can diminish the tragedies described in the reports but by this publication we may at least help to prevent other children sharing the same fate.

NORMAN FOWLER
Secretary of State for Social Services

Contents

vi

Introduction

Background

The last decade has seen the publication of a series of reports of inquiries into cases of child abuse. Some of the inquiries were set up locally by the authorities involved, others by central government. They were established to assess the effectiveness of welfare services provided, so that weaknesses in procedures and practice could be rectified and good procedures and practice developed. The publication of the reports brought the findings and recommendations to a wide audience.

This study results from many requests by local agencies that DHSS should analyse the reports in order to identify their common lessons for practice. It has been undertaken by the small group of staff in DHSS HQ responsible for advising ministers on policy in relation to the prevention and treatment of child abuse. The group consists of administrators and representatives of the main professional groups involved: social work, nursing and medicine.

Source Material

The reports considered in this study are listed in Appendix I. They have provided the basic material for analysis but we have also been influenced by our previous professional experience and our knowledge of a substantial number of other child abuse cases which have never become the subject of public inquiry.

The reports vary in both form and content. Some set out findings without giving the facts on which they are based; some combine narrative and comment in a way which makes it difficult to separate the two. The ages of the children ranged from 7 months to 19½ years. The type of abuse was in some cases neglect, in others emotional abuse, and in others physical violence; some cases involved more than one kind of abuse. All these factors make comparison and collation difficult.

Method

The nature of the material makes any strictly scientific analysis impossible. References to what we found to be the most commonly recurring or most important issues have simply been grouped together, using direct quotation from the reports to clarify or illustrate individual points. Inevitably, the process of selection will have reflected our own view of what is important, but this does not mean that we have seen the study as an opportunity to present our own ideas on good practice: the aim throughout has been to reproduce as objectively as possible the concerns of the reports themselves. Similarly, it must not be assumed that the Department wholeheartedly endorses everything the reports say.

The Table of Contents shows how the material is organised but the content of the reports does not divide neatly into separate topics. Assessment, decision-making, individual roles, relationships between workers, and so on, form a cluster of inter-connected concepts: there is therefore unavoidable overlap between different sections of the study, and some references appear more than once. Comments on each topic are, however, designed to stand by themselves and cross-references have been kept to a minimum.

Aims

The study concentrates on issues connected with child abuse. But the protection of abused or neglected children is only one element in the statutory provision for the care and protection of children whose parents, for whatever reason, are unable to provide such care, or who are deemed to be in need of supervision, as in certain private fostering arrangements or in placement prior to adoption.

A number of the reports could perhaps more appropriately form part of a study of the exercise by the local authority of its child care and protection responsibilities—notably the Stephen Menheniott, Paul Brown, Maria Colwell and Lester Chapman cases. Indeed, in eleven of the reports, the abused child or a child of the family was or had been in the care of the local authority. We have not examined this area in detail, but it is impossible to separate child abuse and neglect entirely from this wider context and we have not attempted to draw any artificial lines.

The study, then, concentrates on what the reports say about child abuse. We have tried to make it short enough to be read and assimilated by those without time to study all the individual reports, detailed enough to demonstrate how the topics covered relate to practice, and coherent enough to give a clear and helpful picture. We hope that those directly involved in the prevention and treatment of child abuse will find it useful, and that it will also be of interest and relevance to others who are concerned with, or about, the general care and protection of children.

Finally, we would like to record our thanks to the colleagues who have helped in carrying out this study.

Ann de Peyer

Lawrence Eaton

Dorothy Black, *Senior Medical Officer*

Margaret Clough, *Social Work Service Officer*

Daphne Learmont, *Nursing Officer*

Frank Tait, *Senior Medical Officer*

Abbreviations

The following abbreviations are used in referring to individual reports:

CT	Carly Taylor
DC	Darryn Clarke
GB (1)	Graham Bagnall (Social Services Committee Report)
GB (2)	Graham Bagnall (Hospital Management Committee Report)
JA	The Family of John George Auckland
KS	Karen Spencer
LC	Lester Chapman
LG	Lisa Godfrey
MC	Maria Colwell
MM	Maria Mehmedagi
MPE	Malcolm Page
MPI	Max Piazzani
NH	Neil Howlett
PB	Paul Brown
RC	Richard Clark
SMS	Steven Meurs
SMT	Stephen Menheniott
SP	Simon Peacock
WB	Wayne Brewer

Numbers in the references refer to paragraphs, unless otherwise stated.

SECTION 1 Agency Functions

1.1   In the cases studied, as in most child protection work, a number of services were routinely involved. Several others became involved indirectly, or for special reasons. In all, the reports mention some twenty-four different kinds of professional and voluntary worker, including social workers of various agencies, paediatricians, psychiatrists, general practitioners, nurses, police, education department staff, and housing department staff (Appendix 2). With so many involved, issues arise concerning agency functions. A clear understanding of the effect that the prescribed or permitted functions of an agency have upon the work of those employed in it is important, since professionals with the same basic professional orientation and training may have very different parts to play, depending on the objectives and responsibilities of their employing agency. For example, social workers in a voluntary organisation may share a common base of professional skills and knowledge with social workers in a Social Services Department or the probation service, but their agencies have different responsibilities. The reports demonstrate that problems can arise where there is lack of clarity about the different contributions of the various agencies and individuals involved. Problems can also arise when a particular worker is asked to fulfil several different roles which are not clearly distinguished. Finally there are problems of overlap where particular functions are held in common by more than one agency.

1.2   Agency functions are to a very large extent shaped, if not actually determined, by the law. It may therefore be helpful to begin by giving a brief account of the relevant statutory provisions and the thinking underlying them, before going on to consider the inquiries' comments on the functions of individual agencies in child care and protection, on problems concerning their interrelation (particularly in the context of case conferences), and on the agencies' roles in relation to the courts and the legal framework.

Statutory provision

1.3   The 1933 and 1969 Children and Young Persons Acts contain the main provisions relating to the care and protection of children who are being abused, or are at risk of abuse. These provisions specify the circumstances in which children may be removed from their parents or supervised in their own home. Some measures are designed to cover emergencies, others to safeguard children's welfare on a longer-term basis.

1.4   The thinking which underlies the statutory provisions, and which was clearly set out in the report of the Curtis Committee*, is that responsibility for affording care and protection should rest with a single agency—the local authority, acting in most instances through its Social Services Committee and Department. The police and the National Society for the Prevention of Cruelty to Children both have certain powers of intervention, and these, together with the local authority, we therefore call the child protection agencies. Only the local authority, however, is bound by a statutory duty both to investigate allegations of abuse and to bring care proceedings, where it considers intervention warranted.

1.5   These points are discussed in more detail in Appendix 3. The reports show how important it is that all workers who may have to deal with child abuse should understand in broad terms the legal framework and its implications for their work; there are, for example, instances of errors by health workers as well as social workers caused by ignorance of the law. Those having to operate the provisions more directly need more detailed knowledge.

Individual agencies

1.6   It must be remembered that what follows is derived from reports of inquiries and therefore relates specifically to work in the child care and protection field, even though many of the points apply to particular agencies' functions in all areas of their activity.

Social Services Departments (SSDs)

1.7   The Graham Bagnall report states the basic position, that the local authority is the main agent for the care and protection of children. As such, it should be kept informed through its SSD of events and developments relating to the child's welfare and protection by all other agencies (GB(1) 37, 38). The Maria Colwell report points out that children who come

---

* Report of the Care of Children Committee, September 1946. HMSO Cmnd 6922

to the attention of other agencies may, unknown to those agencies, already be under some form of supervision by the SSD because of concern about the child's welfare and the SSD may have information to support those agencies' concern (MC 92, 117). (Other references: MM 142(b); SMS 6.10).

1.8 The SSD, as a department of a local authority, has responsibilities to the local community as a whole as well as to the individuals it is designed to help. The Darryn Clarke inquiry recognised that in seeking to establish an objective assessment of need social workers must cultivate an awareness of the feelings and perceptions of the individual and of the complexities of family relationships; they need to accept people as they are and to avoid making judgments or imposing alien solutions. "However, social workers have other responsibilities towards society which employs them. These responsibilities are prescribed by the standards of behaviour which society accepts, the type of services or methods of help it is prepared to provide, and the law it enacts. Social workers can therefore be seen as agents of both care and control" (DC 174). The inquiry commented further "An appreciation of the complexities of the social worker's task is important to a clear understanding of the responsibility of SSDs for children, particularly children who are at risk of injury or neglect, for it is in this field that skill and experience is at a premium, legal requirements are precisely drawn, and public concern most frequently focussed" (DC 175).

1.9 The Auckland report comments further on the theme of "care and control": "the statutory functions of the social services are defined in many Acts and are impossible to encapsulate. They embrace....individuals and groups of all ages with special caring and protective responsibilities for children. Our conception of the responsibility of social workers is to contribute to the prevention of personal distress by the early identification of need, to provide support and help to clients within their homes, to arrange, where necessary, day or residential care, and to intervene, within statutory powers, where the client's own safety or that of others demands it" (JA 31). The report goes on "it is the responsibilities arising out of these powers and duties which probably give rise to the most complex and stressful situations with which social workers have to deal and which call for a high degree of professional skill, experience and judgment" (JA 32).

1.10 The Paul Brown inquiry put the matter very directly: "Whilst a SSD exists to help people in trouble or difficulty it must be emphasized that in respect of children the Department is also a protection agency and the rights of the parent must always be balanced against the need to protect the child...We would wish to draw attention to the rights of children to be protected from those parents who, for whatever reason, expose their children to influences which impair their proper development" (PB 105). (Other references: LC 173; MPE 3.22).

1.11   Despite the SSD's central function in child care and protection, and despite its role of representing the community's values, the Darryn Clarke inquiry found that Darryn's family appeared to have had "little knowledge of the role of the SSD with regard to children found in the position Darryn occupied" (DC 29). The inquiry suggested that the SSD had a role to play in publicising information about child abuse and the help available, or at least about its own functions and responsibilities (DC 194).

National Society for the Prevention of Cruelty to Children (NSPCC)
1.12   Much of the legislation relating to the care and protection of children in the post-Curtis Committee period was based on the principle of undivided responsibility, to ensure that children in need of care and protection should not fall through the net of various agencies or departments of the same agency. Put more simply, it was to be clearly laid down "where the buck stops". However, the NSPCC retained certain powers, such as the power to take care proceedings, alongside those of the then Children's Departments because of the Society's long history in the field of child protection and the widespread public recognition of the agency's function which is incorporated in its title. In fact, by some the Society is still seen as the main agency in this field. The Maria Colwell inquiry acknowledged that "there is every reason to suppose that, largely for historical reasons, complaints commonly reach the NSPCC rather than the SDD". The panel heard from witness upon witness that it was to the NSPCC, "the cruelty people" as they are known, that people naturally turned when they wished to complain about children at risk (MC 187). (Other reference: DC 29).

1.13   In the light of the NSPCC's public standing and partial overlap with the SSD's functions, the Maria Colwell inquiry addressed itself to the broader question of the "advantages and disadvantages of having in existence two parallel services, one voluntary, one statutory, for the detection and investigation of complaints" (MC 189). One advantage, which the inquiry agreed carried weight, was the independence of the voluntary organisation to "go it alone" if need be. Two further possible arguments for a parallel service, which the inquiry felt were less clear, were the fact that the public *do* approach the NSPCC and that the resources of SSDs were stretched to the limit. The inquiry concluded that "this does not mean that the present policy of...providing an alternative channel is a rational use of resources which are scarce both in the voluntary and statutory sector" (MC 189).

1.14 The Maria Colwell inquiry recognised the value of the experimental work being undertaken by the NSPCC, in particular the setting up of specialised units for treatment, but distinguished these welcome developments from "routine work which results in two social workers acting in a similar capacity over a particular case or in a given geographical area". Acknowledging that this situation was not one which could be changed quickly, it comments that "if the NSPCC is considering a long term shift of emphasis it might be to the benefit of children at risk both by the avoidance of duplication and by the development of specialised treatment and research in the NSPCC" (MC 191). (Other reference: DC 214, 216).

1.15 NSPCC workers also meet problems arising out of the dual functions of care and control (see paragraphs 1.8 – 1.10). Their position is slightly different in that by law they are empowered, rather than required, to act but in practice the Society has elected to impose duties on its staff similar to those laid on local authorities by statute.

Police

1.16 A number of the reports demonstrate the frequency of police involvement in situations which indicate the possibility of child abuse or neglect. In the Darryn Clarke case, the police were approached directly by family members who could not locate the child and were concerned about possible illtreatment. In a few other cases, the police were called in when children had been left alone (Maria Colwell, Neil Howlett, Steven Meurs) or to incidents of domestic violence or fracas with neighbours (the Auckland children, Maria Colwell, Richard Clark), and the police became involved in picking up Lester Chapman when he ran away.

1.17 Although the DHSS and the Home Office have subsequently issued guidance on co-operation between the police and other agencies in child abuse cases,* it remains relevant to quote the Maria Colwell report's comments on the need for the police to communicate with other relevant agencies, especially the SSD as the main agency. There were two occasions, "crucial to the welfare of Maria", when the police became involved (although not directly because of Maria herself) and made no referral to the SSD (MC 195). In relation to the specific issue of children left alone the inquiry suggested that the police should play safe in passing on all infor-

---

* "Non-Accidental Injury to Children: The Police and Case Conferences." (LASSL(76)26/HN(76)50/Home Office Circular 179/76.

mation about incidents to which they have been called, leaving it to the SSDs to decide, on the basis of the extent of their knowledge of the case and the seriousness of the incident, what action, if any, to take (MC 198).

1.18   The Wayne Brewer report refers to the special role and skills of the police in the investigation of crime. The report suggests that if they had been involved, the police might have obtained evidence, otherwise lacking, which would have secured the child's removal. "The police have special skills in investigation which might have yielded the vital evidence to justify either removal of the child to a place of safety, or application for an order placing the child in the care of the Council" (WB 12.2). The report acknowledges that bringing in the police might have jeopardised the link the social workers had patiently built with the parents and that whether the intervention of the police will be in the interests of a child is a matter of professional judgment. The report nevertheless recommends that the police "should be asked to intervene directly when their investigative skills could provide important information not otherwise obtainable" (WB 16.23).

1.19   In the Maria Mehmedagi case the police were involved in the investigation of serious injuries to the child. There was some ill-feeling between the police on the one hand and the doctors and social workers on the other (MM 58) and one factor contributing to this ill-feeling was a lack of appreciation of respective functions. A detective inspector became aware that social workers and some others involved had been discussing allegations with the parents, and told them that any direct interviews with the parents must be carried out by the police. The report makes some useful distinctions between the functions of the police and the other services. "The police must obviously be given every assistance to prepare prosecutions and to ensure that the formalities of taking statements are strictly complied with, as required by the criminal courts. At the same time doctors and social workers also have a duty to consider what should be best for a child who has suffered injuries" (MM 57). The report distinguishes between "'interviewing' (which may be undertaken by doctors and social workers) to obtain a medical and social history on which to base the best treatment and care of the child, and 'questioning' (which may be undertaken by police) as to causation and fault regarding the injuries" (MM 58).

1.20   As a means of reducing the likelihood of misunderstandings between the police and welfare agencies in cases of child abuse, the Maria Mehmedagi report draws attention to the importance of the role played by Juvenile Bureaux where they exist. "In our view, if the CID are actively engaged in a case as here, they should automatically inform their Juvenile

Bureau where the referral has not come from that bureau. Juvenile Bureau officers have a responsibility in child and family matters. It was their absence from this case in its formative period which increased the antipathy between the police and other agencies" (MM 78). Not all police forces operate Juvenile Bureaux, of course, but the general lesson is the same: the need to develop close liaison with welfare agencies, based on mutual understanding of each other's functions.

Health Services
1.21   The health services have a responsibility for health education, health surveillance, prevention, diagnosis and treatment and this responsibility extends to the whole community. In the field of child abuse they have a more specific function, for not only must they provide specialist advice and opinion but also they may be required to provide and evaluate evidence for the court if legal action is being considered. The reports' comments on the health services demonstrate the complexity of health service roles, due in part to the variety of the services and the different functions and specialties of health service practitioners. The universality of the health services makes it likely that at some level the health services will be involved in every case of child abuse. This indicates their value as potential sources of information to all other agencies, and confers on all health service staff a particular responsibility to keep others informed. For example, the consultant paediatrician, general practitioner, medical officer of health and health visitor all knew that John Roy Auckland was being discharged from hospital to a household where a previous child had been killed, yet none informed the local authority children's department (JA 109). There were similar failures of communication in the Graham Bagnall case (GB(1) 20, 23) and Malcolm Page case (MPE 4.17). At the same time the Wayne Brewer report recognises that other professions have a responsibility to keep health workers informed: "it is for the Social Worker to keep Consultant Paediatricians apprised of any changes affecting his social circumstances or as in this case of proposed court proceedings" (WB 6.11).

1.22   Reports also refer to the need for health workers to communicate effectively among themselves. For example, the Maria Mehmedagi report says "We consider it absolutely vital that where a hospital suspects child abuse such suspicion should be referred to on the discharge note and in all cases copies of the discharge note should be sent as quickly as possible to the general practitioner and health visitor" (MM 31). (Other references PB 140; CT 86).

1.23   The Maria Colwell report draws attention to the importance of medical assessment as a baseline for monitoring progress. Had Maria continued to have regular medical examinations, the steady deterioration in her emotional and physical state would have been picked up. "A prerequisite of the value of such examinations is, of course, the initial examination at the moment of a child's return home, with its vital baseline data. We think that not only might such provisions have averted Maria's tragedy but that their value in similar cases is clear" (MC 236). The Malcolm Page report also discusses the importance of health monitoring in child abuse cases (see Section 2, paragraphs 2.28, 2.29).

1.24   The *consultant paediatrician* may be the most consistent figure in continuing surveillance of the child. In the Wayne Brewer case, for example, he had been involved from shortly after the birth of the child (WB 6.5), while throughout the life of the child four social workers, two health visitors and four general practitioners were involved at some point. The paediatrician may have not only a specific role in continuing supervision but by virtue of this may offer advice on management of the case. When Maria Mehmedagi had been in hospital for four months, with minimal visiting by her mother, the hospital expressed concern about her lack of stimulation, and the consultant later wrote urging fostering as soon as possible—"but no one treated this as a matter of urgency and insufficient efforts were made" (MM 74).

1.25   The Auckland report mentions difficulties experienced by the consultant paediatrician over confidentiality. "She followed the traditional principles of confidentiality adopted by the medical profession and would only pass on to others such medical information as was necessary for the interest of the patient, and then only to other medical colleagues" (JA 108). The inquiry recommended that "doctors working in hospitals...should be able to recognise evidence [of an 'at risk' situation] and should at once notify the social services, probably through the medical social worker" (JA 254). (Other reference: GB (2) 8).

1.26   Another hospital specialist who may be involved is the *psychiatrist,* although he is more likely to be involved with the parents, either before or after the risk to the child is recognised. However, the need for effective communication remains. The Auckland inquiry states it is the duty of a consultant to whom referral has been made to notify the GP or other referring consultant, if he loses contact with the patient (JA 252). The consultant when writing his report to the general practitioner "should do so in terms which the GP can reasonably be expected to understand, and not use the letter simply as an aide memoire for his own future use" (JA 253).

1.27 The Maria Colwell report underlines the function of the psychiatrist, and the paediatrician, as a "second opinion" to social services, in certain circumstances. There are overlap areas between the medical and social work professions. "If there is reluctance to seek a second opinion, from another discipline, and too much emphasis is placed on independent judgment, then clients will suffer, as Maria did" (MC 61).

1.28 A further function of psychiatric intervention is suggested later in the Maria Colwell report. "It was suggested in evidence that one reason for referral to a Child Guidance Clinic would have been that it would have given Maria a chance to talk to someone about her feelings....the suggestion of an 'alternative channel'....is important". In some instances because of the conflicting roles of a social worker, they may not be "the person in whom the child would feel able to confide" (MC 215).

1.29 The overlap of functions between psychiatrist and social worker is discussed at length in the Maria Colwell report—the possibility of referring Maria to a Child Guidance Clinic was noted on several occasions, both before and after her removal back to her parents. The majority report suggests that a psychiatric opinion should have been sought: "we appreciate that social work training contains an element of child psychology. Surely, however, such training should enable social workers to turn readily for specialist help when severe trauma presents, so that medical skill can supplement their own casework skill" (MC 60). The social work member of the panel thought, however, that social workers engaged in child care and protection were appointed specifically to deal with situations where children were suffering from stress or traumatic change, as distinct from pathological conditions, and that not only must they have the skills needed in those situations but they actually acquired more expertise and experience in dealing with them (MC 319).

1.30 *General Practitioners* are also commonly involved in child abuse cases and the reports identify their contact with the whole family as a valuable source of knowledge (MM 49; PB 158). However, they may face difficulties in participating in multi-professional work, particularly case conferences: they may be unable to attend because case conferences are often held at short notice when the GP already has commitments in his surgery (MM 49). The GP may also see participation in multi-professional discussions as a breach of confidence with patients (MM 49; MC 138). The Malcolm Page inquiry acknowledged these difficulties and stated "we consider that general medical practitioners have an important part to play in the multi-disciplinary management of cases of child abuse....they should be given every positive encouragement to participate....attention should be given to making invitations to case conferences as specific as possible about the areas of concern in which their help is being sought" (MPE 4.18). The Maria Mehmedagi inquiry suggested that questions of breaking confidence (with patients) were similar to those faced by workers from other professions (MM 49). (Other references: LG 218; MC 151; WB 5.23; KS 2.139, 2.143).

1.31 Reports also draw attention to the need for GPs to communicate effectively with other workers, particularly the health visitor. The Auckland report comments: "We consider that a GP should be able to recognise evidence of a situation where a child might be at risk, and should not hesitate to notify either a health visitor, or the social services, or both" (JA 259). The Paul Brown report expresses concern over the failure of a GP not only to work effectively with the health visitor himself, but also to pass on to her information from the consultant paediatrician (PB 138). Another GP in the case said he had originally been "unclear" about the health visitor's role but had developed a close working relationship and had "learned a great deal from her". His health visitor saw every child on his list, and was notified each week of any alterations to the list (PB 139).

1.32 *Health visitors* were involved in all but one of the cases (Stephen Menheniott) under consideration and the inquiries had much to say on their function. The Steven Meurs report, for example, says: "Their functions include the early detection of ill-health and the surveillance of high risk groups, the giving of advice as to the care of young children and the prevention of mental, physical and emotional ill-health. The health visitor has, however, no right of entry into other people's homes, but she calls both on her own initiative as well as when asked to do so" (SMS 11.05).

1.33 Because health visitors call routinely, the Auckland report points out that in cases concerning children under five a social worker may assume the involvement of a health visitor, but not vice versa. The onus therefore lies on the social worker to establish contact (JA 114). And because health visiting covers the whole population, not just those with particular needs or problems, the Peacock inquiry suggested that the character of the health visitor's involvement with families differed from that of social workers (SP p.16, 4.2). As a result the health visitor may acquire information about families which is inaccessible to others. As the minority Maria Colwell report puts it, "Few people hear more than a health visitor!" (MC 293). (Other reference: MPE 4.20).

1.34   The Malcolm Page report discusses the part played by health visitors in child abuse cases at some length. It quotes the Health Visitors' Association Memorandum on Health Visiting and Child Abuse: "Unlike most nurses, Health Visitors work as independent practitioners, accepting individual responsibility for selecting their own priorities and making their own decision within the framework of duties indicated during their training or usually prescribed in outline by their employing authority". The Memorandum goes on to say: "Among the many professional decisions health visitors have to make, one of the most difficult is a firm withdrawal from over-involvement with families which have already reached a crisis of some kind. The function of the Health Visitor is the promotion of good health and hence the prevention of physical, mental or social breakdown and a Health Visitor who gives too much time to one family, already needing remedial help of any kind, is inevitably failing to visit other families..... When remedial help is needed the Health Visitor should refer the family to the appropriate source of continuing support, usually a doctor, nurse or social worker" (MPE 2.37 et seq). The report interprets the Memorandum as saying that Health Visitors exercise their functions by giving advice and responding to requests for advice rather than by being directive or interventionist. A distinction is seen between the preventive work of health visitors and the remedial work of social workers. "We do not think that in practice such a clear cut distinction is possible and there is bound to be overlap. Hence the need in any particular case for the social worker and the health visitor to be very clear about what each is expecting the other to do" (MPE 4.19).

Education

1.35   Another service likely to be involved in the welfare of families with school age children is the Education Welfare Service. With few exceptions, Education Departments rather than Social Services Departments have responsibility for this service. This division was seen by the Maria Colwell Inquiry as being *one* factor, amongst others, which made it more difficult for the concern of the Education Welfare Officer (EWO) about Maria to reach the SSD. At no time were the EWO and the SSD officer supervising Maria in contact and the inquiry was much concerned about the liaison between the two services. Since it is "generally accepted" that the EWO's task "should go beyond concern for regular school attendance and extend to more general issues of welfare", the report hopes that "every effort will be made to ensure direct and frequent communication between the social workers in the Social Services Department and the education welfare officers" (MC 185).

1.36　The EWO in the Maria Colwell case showed admirable persistence in the pursuit of Maria's welfare but "was operating in isolation from the other social services" (MC 141). She "suffered an apparent confusion of thought over her role". She was confused "in her dual role as an education welfare officer in the sense that her initial enquiries were directed to non-attendance at school and that these led on to consideration of the general welfare aspect of Maria's case"; she may have communicated some of this confusion to the GP whom she had put in the picture as to her fears for Maria's welfare. The doctor advised that Maria could attend school and when the EWO mentioned the possibility of court action the GP agreed to supply a report if the case came to court. Neither party, however, appears to have been clear what action was to be taken and for what purpose (MC 138).

1.37　There was "some division of responsibility for the noting and refer-ring" of matters of concern about children "between the teachers and the school secretaries" (MC 175). Also, the role and status of the EWO within the school was uncertain (MC 176).

1.38　The part played by the teachers and staff at the schools Maria attended is discussed. The report accepts that a headmaster has "the ulti-mate responsibility" for the welfare of his pupils, but sees it as "essential....that the class teacher is always involved, preferably through direct contact with the social worker concerned". The panel were impressed by the sincerity and perceptiveness of all three of Maria's class teachers, but felt that on occasion "anxieties about Maria's situation might have been conveyed with greater accuracy and urgency" (MC 174). The panel also pointed to the potential importance of the school secretary as a communication link between schools, if a child moves as Maria did (MC 175).

Probation

1.39　Probation officers have a wide range of duties to persons who are subject to probation or supervision orders, or to licence following release from prison, detention centres or borstal, or to voluntary aftercare. These duties include work with juveniles as well as adults. Probation officers may be concerned with abusing families because of an offence not directly related to children's welfare, as in the Lisa Godfrey case, or where a parent has been convicted of some form of ill-treatment or neglect, as in the Maria Mehmedagi case. They also have particular responsibilities for the provision of reports to courts in criminal and matrimonial proceedings.

1.40   Where the probation officer's supervisory or reporting duty arises out of an offence or circumstances directly related to the welfare of the family, then the extent of that duty may have to be interpreted widely. The probation officer in the Maria Mehmedagi case told the inquiry "that she regarded her main professional and statutory responsibility as seeing father, and although she would expect to work closely with other members of the family, her oversight of Maria would take into account that the child was in the care of social services". The report comments that although during the social workers' strike both the probation officer and health visitor were seeing the family, they had no common understanding of what each was visiting for. The result was that "no one had a commitment to see Maria on home visits" (MM 100). (Other reference: CT 59).

1.41   Even in cases where the offence or circumstances occasioning the probation officer's involvement are not related to the family's welfare, the reports indicate that a clear understanding of roles and responsibilities is important. Lisa Godfrey's mother was on probation for an unrelated offence and there was an identified risk of child abuse. The SSD, albeit reluctantly, dropped out of the case, at the express wish of the probation officer. But the inquiry considered that the SSD could not delegate its statutory duty to give care and protection to Lisa, and therefore it continued to have a role. The report says "there should have been a clarification, preferably at senior officer level, of what were the implications of the resultant decision that the Probation Officer would retain the responsibility for family casework and that the Social Services Directorate would take no action except on further request....there was no recognition of implicit delegation (in the absence of explicit delegation) of certain local authority responsibilities to the Probation and After Care Service. In consequence, there were no agreed arrangements for joint consideration of future developments and plans" (LG 181).

Relationships between Agencies
1.42   The need for a clear understanding of the principles of multi-professional work is well illustrated in all the reports. The Lester Chapman inquiry observed that there is a tendency, "when many persons have duties in relation to one family, for responsibility to become blurred and decisions avoided and for vital information to be lost sight of or overlooked" (LC p.66, xiii). The following paragraphs draw together what the reports

say about the interrelationships between agencies and professions and how they may cause such problems.

1.43   The workers whose functions are most frequently described as being insufficiently known to others are health visitors and social workers, but others are mentioned. The Max Piazzani inquiry, for example, was "advised by the representatives of each discipline that in their view they were not adequately informed of the responsibilities of the other disciplines and to some extent this was apparent in this case" (MPI p.12, 28). In addition to lack of understanding, the Wayne Brewer report, in a discussion of case conferences, refers to the tendency of professionals to assume "erroneously" that they know what each other's contribution will be (WB 5.21.). (Other references: MM 39; WB 6.11; SMS 11.05; DC 165; MC 150; PB 139, 140; JA 259).

1.44   As well as drawing attention to differences of function, the Darryn Clarke report points out that "the extent of the relevant authorities' involvement in and commitment to cases of non-accidental injury to children and child abuse differs considerably". For the police, child abuse forms only a small part of their duties (DC 149). The incident at the police station in the Lester Chapman case, referred to in Section 2 (paragraph 2.58), also illustrates this distinction between extent and nature of involvement. The social worker had to consider the care and protection of the child and decide whether to intervene in his interests. The police had to consider these matters too but also had to decide whether a criminal offence had been committed and whether a charge should be brought (LC 180).

Separate viewpoints
1.45   Workers will have a different view of the world according to their agency's function and their particular skills and knowledge. The Colwell report recognised this problem saying "it was apparent to us that the definition of a so-called 'problem family' may vary according to the frame of reference of the agency" (MC 193). Social workers, in particular, work with a population which is often beset with many problems and stresses, and may take a less serious view of certain circumstances than workers involved with the population as a whole. There is a danger, as pointed out in the Malcolm Page report (MPE 3.112), that when the worker is constantly exposed to a deprived population standards will be adjusted downwards to an unacceptable level. The views of those not so exposed may therefore provide a useful corrective, since there will inevitably be occasions where judgments will differ. The health visiting service, for instance, is a universal

one, and what may appear as deviating from the "normal" to a health visitor may not do so to a social worker.

Duplicate functions

1.46   It is interesting to note that in eight of the cases in this study both SSD and NSPCC (or RSSPCC) were involved at some stage of the story. In seven of the cases (Darryn Clarke, Maria Colwell, Richard Clark, Lester Chapman, Neil Howlett, Graham Bagnall, Steven Meurs) both agencies were involved at the same time. The question of relationships between the local authority and the NSPCC features prominently in the Maria Colwell report. It was the NSPCC who originally removed Maria from home on a Place of Safety Order and returned her to the care of her aunt and uncle. This placement had implications for the later decision of the local authority, to whose care she was committed, to leave her there. It demonstrates the way in which the care authority's exercise of its responsibilities can be subtly affected by the actions of other agencies. It was, says the minority report, "an unusual procedure. There was not full consultation between the NSPCC and the Children's Department before this was done, as there should have been since it is not part of the NSPCC's task to place children" (MC 254).

1.47   The Darryn Clarke inquiry also drew attention to possible adverse effects upon the family of such duplication of functions. The NSPCC inspector contended that "a visit to a family by three representatives of authority following an allegation of non-accidental injury to a child, whether they visited together or separately, might well have caused distress or antagonism, or otherwise cause or accelerate the process they were striving to prevent." His agency had therefore passed on the referral to the SSD, although this did not accord with the NSPCC's procedures. The panel felt there was some merit in this and recommended that this point should be considered by the Society (DC 221).

1.48   The Maria Colwell inquiry pointed out, in the context of relations between the SSD and NSPCC, that willingness to co-operate by itself is not enough. Because of the good working relationship between the two agencies the respective workers in the case did not formalise their roles or double check that all necessary steps had been taken. The consequent blurring of roles, together with the fact that both were overworked, "increased the chances of each depending too heavily on the other to spot trouble" (MC 188). "At the very least", the inquiry concluded, consultations at senior level were needed "to set guidelines for the conduct of cases in which

both agencies might be involved.... Where social workers from different
agencies decide to co-operate on the same case, the plan should be
confirmed in writing and their respective seniors informed" (MC 189).

1.49 The Darryn Clarke report also considers the question of clear, agreed
guidelines where functions overlap. A suggestion was put to the inquiry that
the NSPCC "should deal with all cases of suspected or actual non-
accidental physical injury, as distinct from cases of child abuse, notified by
the public to the Society or referred on to the Society by the police.... The
Society's funds were limited and they could not deal with all non-accidental
injury cases, let alone cases of child abuse, arising in the Liverpool area."
However the inquiry considered this proposal "so specialised as to give rise
to a grave risk that cases will fall between the Social Services and the
Society" (DC 222). In relation to a proposed procedure for passing
information from the police to the SSD and NSPCC the inquiry emphasised
the necessity of indicating which agency was receiving the referral for action
and which for information. "The risk of a complaint 'falling between two
stools' is obvious, grave, and must be guarded against" (DC 226). (Further
material relating to this risk will be found in paragraph 2.60.)

Case Conferences
1.50 The case conference has long held a central place in child abuse procedures as a means of structuring communication and collaboration. It provides a forum where a full exchange of information can take place and the
actions of the various agencies can be co-ordinated. However, the reports
suggest that the case conference may often not be used to maximum
advantage. All the inquiry reports, either implicitly or more often explicitly,
highlight critical occasions when a case conference could have had a
significant effect on the way a case was handled but either was not held at
all or was ineffective for one reason or another. In the case of Wayne
Brewer, "the network of communications...was good and so a case
conference was not seen as necessary" (WB 2.46). But the report goes on to
point out that "case discussions between individuals or small groups of
officers are not an adequate substitute when the occasion demands a case
conference" (WB 5.20). Failure to convene a conference after the care
order was revoked and Wayne returned to his parents meant that no formal
plan of management was drawn up (WB 5.7); and failure to convene a
conference after Wayne's second injury meant that no one considered
involving the police (WB 5.18).

1.51 The Malcolm Page report defined the purposes of a case conference as

"—to share knowledge about the family as a whole including its history and information about individual members

—to try to diagnose the problem and assess the family, including the degree of risk of abuse to which *all* of the children within the family are exposed

—to allocate the case to a key worker responsible for its overall management

—to recommend to the key worker and others to whom responsibility falls or is assigned a treatment plan

—to decide whether or not to register any of the children" (MPE 5.9). (Other references: LC p.66, xiv; NH p.16, 5).

1.52 The Maria Mehmedagi report stresses that a full social history, provided by the social worker, should be considered by the case conference. The history should cover "the social and medical history of the parents, their attitude, and information about the extended family both on the father's side and the mother's side" (MM 142(b)). The agenda for the meeting should "specify clearly all the options available, from immediate return home without further surveillance to court action with a view to a care order and to long term fostering or adoption" (MM 142(c)).

1.53 In itself, however, the case conference is no more than a tool. The inquiries have pointed out two main areas where proficiency is essential if the conference is to achieve its purposes. The first is the chairing of the conference. The Wayne Brewer report says "we think that the results yielded by the case conference can be greatly enhanced and more speedily achieved by skilful chairmanship" (WB 5.24). (Other references: LC 105; PB 157). The Malcolm Page report refers to the need for training in chairmanship (MPE 5.13). The second essential is to record proceedings fully and accurately (WB 16.15; MPE 5.10; MM 142 (e) & (f)) and to ensure that copies of the record go to everyone with an interest, even if not at the conference (KS 3.35; SP p.16, 4.4).

1.54 The reports also comment on who should attend case conferences. The Simon Peacock and Karen Spencer reports provide examples of case conferences which were ineffective because not everyone with a potential contribution to make was present and a full exchange of information was not achieved. The neighbouring authority was not invited to the second case conference on Simon Peacock and so did not appreciate the urgency of the situation when shortly afterwards the family moved back to their area (SP p.16, 4.4). The first case conference on Karen Spencer appears to have endorsed a plan of action that included allowing regular home visits without the benefit of information from her GP, who, although invited, did not attend the conference (KS 2.54 et seq). Neither the GP nor the police attended the third case conference and the consultant psychiatrist was not invited (KS 2.143 et seq). (Other references: PB 158; WB 5.23; MPE 3.101).

1.55 It follows from the importance of proper attendance that due regard must be paid to the issuing of invitations. The police did not attend the first case conference on Maria Mehmedagi and her family because the invitation was not received in time, having been sent by second class post. The report comments "we do find this procedure rather extraordinary. If a case conference has to be called at short notice then courtesy and prudence would indicate that invitees should be informed by telephone. Written notification could well be sent as a follow-up" (MM 76). In discussing the attendance of GP's at case conferences the Malcolm Page report also suggests that invitations should be as specific as possible about the areas of concern in which help is being sought (MPE 4.18).

1.56 Perhaps the most difficult issue is to decide when case conferences should be called. Several reports warn of the dangers of overuse (WB 5.20; PB 157; LC 105), but few offer any explicit criteria for calling them. The Darryn Clarke report suggests "The question of whether a case conference should replace case discussion is a matter involving careful consideration and professional judgement. The review of the guidelines governing the calling of such conferences are [sic] peculiarly within the terms of reference of Area Review Committees" (DC 235). (Other references: MPE 5.14; MPI 20(c)). The Simon Peacock report draws attention to the value of conferences when cases are being handed over to another authority. These should be convened by the receiving SSD and attended by workers from the previous area, if possible, or else supplied with copies of *all* the available information, not just a summary letter (SP p.20, 6.5).

1.57 Lastly, several reports make the point that notwithstanding their vital co-ordinating role, case conferences can only put forward recommendations, and not binding executive instructions. The Simon Peacock report says, "Decisions reached at a case conference should reflect the agreed consensus of those with direct responsibility for implementing them. [But] each constituent authority retains responsibility according to its duties, and it cannot discharge its responsibility by delegating it to a case conference" (SP p.15, 3.4). (Other references: MM 142(b); LC p.66, xiv; PB 159).

The Authority of the Law and the Role of the Courts

1.58   The authority to intervene between parents and their children is rooted in the law and in powers which derive from decisions of the courts. Before any compulsory intervention can take place, other than in the short term, a medical and/or social diagnosis of abuse has to be tested in court. It is for the courts to hear and weigh evidence, to adjudicate between conflicting views and interests and to make decisions which are binding not only on the family but on child protection agencies and others. The courts can only exercise their function in respect of cases that are brought to their attention and can only make decisions on the basis of the evidence put before them.

1.59   This review has not attempted an exhaustive study of the quite extensive comment made by the inquiries on the law and legal matters. In any case, the law itself has changed since some of the reports were written (some important changes are listed in Appendix 4). We have restricted ourselves in the main to a consideration of the reports' findings as they affect the roles and practice of workers: for example, in what circumstances the law should be invoked, what considerations are involved in doing so and what implications there are for workers' relationships with clients.

The Use of Authority

1.60   There are a number of references to the fears of workers struggling to engage the co-operation of parents, that authoritative intervention to protect the child might lead to the breakdown of any relationship they might have established with the parents. The Lester Chapman report refers in its conclusions to the balancing acts which those involved in health and social work, especially social work with children, have to engage in. "The need to establish and maintain a relationship of confidence with the parents may be difficult, perhaps impossible, to reconcile with the workers' duty to the child" (LC p.65, ix). (Other references: MPI 18(b), 20(f); JA 121).

1.61   But whilst the untimely imposition of authority can estrange parents, failure to impose authority and to set limits, as in the Malcolm Page case, can lead to a situation where a case "drifts" (MPE 3.67 et seq.) Here "a failure to exercise appropriate authority and control and immediately to specify and ensure minimal acceptable standards of care for the children left the parents unclear about what was expected of them. The problem was compounded subsequently by a failure to define and agree with Mr and Mrs Page those standards". This failure "to insist upon acceptable standards being maintained became a repeated feature of the case management" (MPE 3.22). Later, after the children were committed to care and placed home on trial, the report stresses the SSD's continuing obligation to see that home conditions were satisfactory and the rights that followed from that responsibility, including the right to inspect the house and to require medical examinations and visits to the clinic. "It is, however one thing to have the right but it is another thing to enforce it against the wishes of the parents. It can be done by removing the child" unless certain requirements are met (MPE 5.21). Whilst acknowledging the difficult casework decisions involved, the inquiry thought "that the solution lies in simply not taking 'No' for an answer and the exercise of personal or statutory authority by the workers involved with the case. . . . . The existing law provides the means to set a specific requirement which if not met can result in the removal of the child" (MPE 5.22).

1.62 The authority of the law can only be properly invoked when there is sound knowledge of the law and also of legal requirements, such as what will be admissible as evidence. The Paul Brown inquiry was concerned "at the general impression given by [SSD's] witnesses regarding their knowledge of the law" and "heard of one social worker who had been in post for a very short time and admitted to having no real knowledge of child care law. Quite senior officers had no knowledge of wardship as a method of protecting children". The inquiry expressed the view that all professional training courses for social workers should have a considerable input of general law and of the law relating to children (PB 60). It also discussed the importance of good liaison between SSD and Local Authority Legal Departments, sugggesting that the responsibility for advising a SSD on child care legislation should be given to a senior solicitor with a particular knowledge of, and interest in, the care of children. It stressed the importance of legal advice being available in the event of emergencies. (Other references: RC 56, 67; LC 58; SP p14, 2.9, 2.10, 4.15; MC 238).

1.63 There are also numerous instances of failure to exercise legal authority held. The supervision of children boarded out in foster homes, for example, is prescribed in Boarding Out Regulations, which set out minimum standards of frequency of visits, medical examinations and reviews. These regulations were breached in respect of visiting (PB 85, 88; LC 50, 59), medical examinations (KS 2.87), and reviews (PB 85, 90; MC 107, 109; SMT 5.15). There are also instances of inadequate supervision where a Supervision Order was in force (MC 107; LC 83). The implication of this and the preceding paragraph is that workers must realise what authority they could have, and be prepared to exercise what authority they do have, at any stage of a case. (Other reference: SMT 2.53).

The Courts

1.64   Paragraph 1.58 referred to the testing by the courts of medical and social diagnosis. Preparing and giving evidence can provide a useful discipline in reaching clear judgments and decisions; the value is, of course, lost to those who prejudge what the court's findings will be. In the Lester Chapman case, for example, a social worker was influenced against seeking a Place of Safety Order partly by a Court's earlier decision to refuse a Care Order in what had seemed a clear case to the SSD (LC 171). In the Maria Colwell case social workers judged, in the legal and social context of the time, that application by the mother for revocation of the care order would succeed within a short time. The inquiry accepted that they were probably right to assume that the magistrates would return the child home once the parents' fitness was proved, unless it could be clearly shown that it would not be in her best interests. When the mother pressed ahead with her application, the local authority, seeking to retain some control in the situation, decided not to oppose it. The effect of the decision was: "because there was no opposition....there was no examination by way of argument or evidence of any reasons why the care order should not be revoked.... The revocation went through virtually 'on the nod'". If opposed, "there would undoubtedly have been a very full hearing with evidence and argument on both sides and the court would have made its decision after every possible point had been taken". The care authority would also have looked "for evidence to justify their opposition" (MC 226), ie this would have imposed a useful discipline on social workers to seek evidence supporting actions. (Other references: KS 2.124, 2.128; WB 4.18).

1.65   Courts test evidence by setting parties against each other. The Wayne Brewer report discusses the advantages and disadvantages of the adversarial system and the appropriateness of the Magistrates Courts as a forum for discussions about the future and safety of children (WB 4.27). It concludes that while the adversarial system can lead to a polarisation of the issues in which the case is seen as a contest "won" or "lost" by the parents or the local authority, in cases where the liberty of individuals is at stake the system allows evidence to be tested rigorously. The inquiry remained "in two minds" as to whether the system is flexible enough to be adapted to the adjudication of issues such as these and suggested that a careful comparison could usefully be made with the Scottish Juvenile Panel system* of the way

---

* For further information see: "Fact Sheet No 7—Children's Hearings." Scottish Information Office; or "Children's Hearings: Notes on Part III of the Social Work (Scotland) Act 1968." HMSO, 1970

in which care proceedings are conducted under each system and of any differences in outcome (WB 4.32). (Other reference: MC 68).

1.66   It is important if all the issues in a case are to be fully explored by the Court, or proceedings are to be brought at all, that evidence is properly collected. A number of reports comment on this point. For example, in the Auckland case, social workers concluded that there were no grounds for instituting care proceedings; the inquiry considered that "at the very least" if the information held by various services had been pooled, by means of a case conference, an application for a care order "would have become a practical possibility" (JA 120). In fact "the available information was not pooled, nor was there any carefully reasoned and documented decision about care proceedings" (JA 122). The Wayne Brewer inquiry referred to the tendency to regard physical injury as the predominant factor in Court proceedings and suggested that local authorities should be more prepared to bring evidence of the likelihood of inquiry and that the courts should be more willing to receive and weigh such evidence (WB 4.25) (see also paragraph 2.58). (Other references: GB(1)20; PB 84; LC p.66, xii).

Reports to the Courts
1.67   The Maria Mehmedagi inquiry found that the probation officer's social enquiry report "was compiled largely from information obtained from the parents, expressing their views and opinions of what took place and hence was heavily weighted in their favour." In other words, the probation officer had "tended to become an advocate for the parents". The inquiry suggested that the report should have given "an accurate and balanced view of the family situation", based on verified fact and relevant background information (MM 87). The Maria Colwell minority report observes that "there is little room for speculative observation in court reports" and also, since it is customary for the parent to see the report, they are "properly cautious". However, "it would have been wise for [the social worker] to air more fully some of the reservations which she had expressed about Maria's step-father in her case records" (MC 309).

1.68   The Wayne Brewer report suggests that "there might well be more occasions on which Magistrates might get definite help from medical and psychiatric reports, if necessary adjourning the proceedings until they are available" (WB 4.34). Where psychiatric reports already exist, they should be tendered as evidence (WB 4.35).

Professional Roles in Court

1.69   The Maria Colwell inquiry described the "plurality of roles" of the social worker in the court context and the difficulties which resulted. The social worker represented the local authority, who were respondents to the application by Maria's mother for revocation of the care order. She also had a duty to prepare an impartial report to the Court, as we have seen, and to carry out the Court's order. In certain circumstances she might also be reasonably expected to adopt the temporary role of advocate. The inquiry recommended that the views of an independent social worker should be available to the Court where the local authority is seeking or consenting to a change in status of a child under their care and supervision and is a party to the proceedings. It was thought this would significantly reduce the problems arising from plurality of roles (MC 227). (See Appendix 4, paragraph 1(a)).

1.70   This conflict of roles in court may be experienced by other professionals, as illustrated by the Karen Spencer report. The consultant psychiatrist received requests for a psychiatric assessment from the local authority social worker and from the parents' solicitor. Both the parents' solicitor and the local authority solicitor were clear that the psychiatrist was the SSD's witness but the Area Officer saw him as giving evidence on behalf of the mother and the Consultant saw himself as acting for the mother (KS 2.118). The report commented that there was no suggestion of impropriety or even confusion but that "there is, I believe, always an element of tension or ambiguity, when a professional (and it can be a lawyer as easily as a medical man or a social worker) owes duties to his client, with whom he will have a continuing relationship, and to the court and other agencies" (KS 2.119).

1.71   The Wayne Brewer report points out the importance of medical practitioners attending court to give evidence in care proceedings. It discusses the reluctance of a consultant paediatrician to appear on grounds of (i) maintaining confidence and observing confidentiality of matters revealed within the doctor/patient relationship; (ii) the time consumed in Court appearances. The report concludes that the closely reasoned case put forward by the SSD against the revocation of the Care Order "would have been broadened by the personal appearance in Court of an experienced Paediatrician able to comment on the child's past condition, his progress and his future needs" (WB 6.17). In its recommendations, it urges medical practitioners "to consider whether time spent in court, even at the expense of other patients in their care, would not be justified where there is a considerable degree of concern about a child" (WB 16.10).

SECTION 2 Professional Practice

2.1 This section looks at the inquiries' comments on a number of aspects of professional practice: the recognition of abuse; the processes of assessment, and of planning and carrying out treatment; and the integral processes of communicating and recording. Some professionals are trained in specific types of assessment or diagnosis, and it is clear that a number of the tasks and skills considered in the reports are the province of particular agencies or professions. However, it is also clear that there are other skills and areas of knowledge which all professionals dealing with child abuse need to acquire and, as the previous section shows, the reports consider it important for multi-professional co-operation that all workers understand the functions and responsibilities of each other's agencies.

2.2 The general picture of practice emerging from the reports is not of gross errors or failures by individuals on single occasions but of a confluence or succession of errors, minor inefficiencies and misjudgements by a number of agencies, together with the adverse effects of circumstantial factors beyond the control of those involved. The Lisa Godfrey report points to the cumulative effect of errors by social, medical, probation and health visiting services (LG 189); in the Carly Taylor case the professionals principally involved were all judged to have worked together to consult, but not to act positively to prevent the tragedy (CT 125); and a witness in the Karen Spencer inquiry described the entire case as "a whole chain of events....strewn with 'if only'" (KS 1.9).

2.3 Because the source material for this study consists of cases where inquiries have been held, mistakes and pitfalls in professional practice tend to be emphasised. No agency escapes criticism but the reports do also refer to, and give examples of, good practice. For instance, the Wayne Brewer report stands out in this respect, and a great deal of good work was identified by the Maria Colwell inquiry; the Auckland inquiry singled out for praise the work of the probation officer over many years (JA 72, 107), and aspects of work done by the social worker, health visitor and consultant psychiatrist in Karen Spencer's case are commended (KS 3.73).

Recognition
2.4   Research has suggested that there are certain social and personal factors associated with child abuse*, but the published reports do not provide the kind of information which would enable us to say whether they were present in these cases.

2.5   There is however, some useful material in the reports about the difficulty of recognising abuse, and also about what the families said or did which might have indicated that children were in danger of, or actually suffering, abuse.

Specialised Knowledge
2.6   Lack of professional experience and expertise in child abuse may lead to failure to identify injury or risk.The significance of a particular factor or cluster of factors may not be appreciated because of lack of knowledge. The Maria Mehmedagi report points to the significance of repeated minor injury such as odd scratches and bruises, especially when associated with signs of poor development and poor parent/child relationships. "All these indications might not individually give cause for great alarm, but collectively they should have been seen as forming a pattern which should have given rise to effective action" (MM 133). The Maria Colwell report identifies the problem of a general practitioner who failed to recognise any particular significance in two small red marks on her cheekbone. The report pointed out that a busy GP might only come across one such presentation of child abuse each year (MC 137). When Mrs Godfrey took Lisa to her general practitioner with severe bruising and a black eye, he did not suspect non-accidental injury. In fact Mrs Godfrey had told him previously that her own deafness had been caused by childhood battering, and he originally thought this would have conditioned her against injuring her children, instead of increasing the risk of her doing so (LG 98).

Blocks to Recognition
2.7   There is a danger that professionals may misconstrue situations by reacting too subjectively or uncritically to one family member. The ·
Auckland report demonstrates very clearly the dangers of accepting too readily one party's account of the situation. "From the start and perhaps

---

* For an account of these factors and a useful bibliography see Chapter 3 of "Violence in the Family": Social Work Services Group, Scottish Education Department. HMSO, 1982.

because of her lack of knowledge of previous events" a social worker "formed an adverse view of Mrs Barbara Auckland and, from this point onwards, the social services' personnel dealing with the Auckland family seem to have been rather too ready to accept information and explanations offered to them by Mr John Auckland and his relations" (JA 149). Another social worker, later in the story, having first talked to Mr Auckland and his parents, went to see Mrs Auckland "with a version of her reasons for leaving her husband already established in his mind"; he "paid comparatively little heed to Mrs Auckland's own complaints about her husband and his family" (JA 190). The social worker succeeded in persuading Mrs Auckland to allow Mr Auckland to have care of the child, at the home of his parents. Susan was subsequently killed by her father, who had previously killed a baby daughter. There were also problems of accepting one party's account too readily in the Maria Mehmedagi case (MM 122) and problems of over-identification with the mother in the Steven Meurs case (SMS 6.02). Fear of manipulation led workers to discount warnings given by the mothers of Paul Brown and Richard Clark (PB 84; RC 40).

2.8   A special type of psychological reaction, denial, may commonly occur where a worker does not wish even to suspect a client of doing something which the worker regards as horrifying. The Darryn Clarke inquiry found that the senior social worker initially believed the source of the problems and complaints lay in the family's disapproval of Darryn's mother's conduct and friends. This caused him not to ask her brother specific questions about the alleged injuries (DC 183) and not to pursue an objective assessment of the situation in the light of new information (DC 184). The senior social worker told the inquiry "he did not want to believe that Darryn was being injured" (DC 184). (Other references: JA 210; SMS 12.06).

2.9   Subjectivity and the confusion of fact and opinion can also distort assessments of a situation. Opinion, if not plainly distinguished, may sometimes pass for "hard" information and therefore go unchallenged despite being ill-founded or inaccurate. The Malcolm Page report refers to "the trap of making statements about conditions without also recording the facts on which those statements are based," and mentions the police description of conditions in the home as a good example of factual reporting. "The message is to record what you actually see otherwise the record can be distorted and lead to decisions based on false assumptions" (MPE 3.110).

Warnings and Signs of Abuse

2.10   Reports identify certain factors which could have alerted workers to the possibility of abuse. Some aspects of the behaviour of the children and adults involved could be seen as attempts to draw attention to, or escape from, their situation.

2.11   Possible warning signs found in the cases are firstly, children being left alone (SMS 7.04; LC 174; MC 117; NH, p.4, entry for 8.5.74), secondly, falling off in school attendance (LC 201; MC 120, 124), and thirdly, failure by professionals to gain access. The Steven Meurs report describes this last factor as a "critical danger signal" (SMS 7.16) and the Carly Taylor report comments "over.....eleven months, during part of which the twins were away, the health visitor made a total of twenty-three visits but on no less than fourteen occasions she was unable to obtain access.....refusal of access to health visitors and the like is one of the well known indicators of potential child abuse and other problems" (CT 48). The Paul Brown inquiry suggested that repeated failure to gain access "should prompt the case worker to check whether other agencies are experiencing the same problem and, where necessary, initiate the appropriate action" (PB 101).

2.12   A child's demeanour may or may not provide a clue. Not all children showed the "frozen awareness" frequently referred to in textbooks. Wayne Brewer suffered "a pretty long history of violence and intimidation" (WB 3.1). Yet when a vigilant social worker visited the family, half expecting to see "a cowering, frightened child" she was instead impressed by the relaxed relationship apparent between Wayne and his stepfather. Wayne "showed no signs of apprehension" (WB 3.3). The consultant paediatrician and health visitor were also deceived by the child's natural resilience (WB 3.12). Similarly, Lester Chapman after being beaten and running away "was not cowed or frightened", but "cheerful" and "revelling in being the centre of attention" (LC 182). Darryn Clarke too, during the period of abuse, was taken to a Safari Park by neighbours and though "initially quiet and subdued" he later became "quite cheerful and showed no signs and made no complaint of soreness" (DC 101). These examples of apparent cheerfulness and well-being may be contrasted with the change of personality in Darryn Clarke noted by the family, who described him as becoming "quiet and withdrawn" rather than "happy, cheeky" and "active" (DC 48); and in Maria Colwell, who at school was showing signs of withdrawal and depression as well as a general deterioration in her appearance, physical and otherwise (MC 111).

2.13 Sometimes children tell someone of abuse directly, though not necessarily a professional. When Paul Brown was in hospital, the nursing record noted he had said "Daddy hits Mummy, also Daddy made sores on left hand with matches". No action was taken but the inquiry suggested that such comments require investigation (PB 79). Darryn Clarke told a friend of his mother's "Charlie had done it" in contradiction to his mother's story that he had fallen downstairs (DC 43). Wayne Brewer told social worker, health visitor and general practitioner that "Daddy did it" (WB 2.62 et seq).

2.14 A child's message may not always be so clear, however, for a variety of reasons, not least because children are inclined to give up if their messages are not well received. The case of Lester Chapman provides one example. He at first told the police quite clearly that he had run away because of being beaten and that he did not want to go home, and that he would run away again (LC 165 – 169). Later on, however, when asked if he wanted to go home he remained silent, and later still he said again that he did not want to go home. After being asked twice what he would do if he did not go home, he agreed to go. After his second running away, he was picked up by the canal and said he was going to jump in (LC 187). His comments then became more oblique. After he ran away for the third time he talked about a programme on TV in which a boy ran away and lived in a tree and said he would like to do that (LC 207). Similarly, Maria Colwell said she would like to live on a farm in the country—"no one would be able to find me there" (MC 53).

2.15 Reports also show that children cannot be relied upon to challenge explanations offered by parents or parent figures, especially when the latter are present. Lisa Godfrey (LG 188(f)), Darryn Clarke (DC 51) and Maria Colwell (MC 88) all endorsed their parents' false explanations. Children do of course fit their response to the expectations of adults, especially those adults who are in a position of power. A social worker is quoted as saying of Maria Colwell, she "chooses what she says knowing what will be acceptable to the person she is addressing" (MC 294). Maria fought against going to visit her mother but appeared to settle down and even enjoy herself once she arrived. On one occasion she ran away and was very distressed but when her mother arrived she calmed down, (although her aunt said she "cringed"), and when taken home was bright and chatty. She "showed no apprehension at all of a comeback from her mother" (MC 306).

2.16 Sometimes children may try to communicate through actions rather than words. Richard Clark's brother "was concerned to show [the social worker] a slight bruise on his leg which he could not tell her how he got" (RC 39). This insignificant gesture has to be seen in a context where the foster parents had a history of ill-treatment and where the child's father had expressed concern that the foster father was "lifting his hand to them". The social worker attached no significance to the child's approach to her (RC 68). Running away featured importantly in the Lester Chapman and Maria Colwell cases. They both ran away several times from their parents, in Lester's case four times in a fortnight. The Maria Colwell report pointed out that such behaviour is very unusual in such young children and the inquiry was not satisfied that it was taken sufficiently seriously (MC 317). Maria was seven and Lester eight. The social worker in the Lester Chapman case also found it unusual, and had never come across it before in a child of Lester's age (LC 189). Its significance as a sympton of disturbance was recognised and steps taken to hasten referral to the Child Guidance Clinic, but the inherent danger of such behaviour was not sufficiently taken into account and Lester died as a result of running away.

2.17   Three reports (Maria Colwell, Stephen Menheniott, Richard Clark) make reference to the extreme importance of direct communication with children and the great difficulty of this with children who have conflicting and fluctuating feelings. Richard Clark, aged 3, had told his great grandmother that he did not want to go home on a number of occasions. His elder brother was in the same private foster home. The inquiry criticised the lack of any attempt at any time by the social workers involved to get the boys to talk about their feelings and discussed the need for specialised knowledge and skill in direct work with children (RC 88, 91). The Maria Colwell report contains an important section on the same subject, in which the need for direct personal communication between social workers and children about their problems is seen as indispensable. The point is also made that, in some instances, children may need an alternative channel to the social worker, who has power to remove them and who may be presented as a threat by parents (MC 209 – 215). The favoured position of schoolteachers, who have a natural opportunity to communicate with children directly, is also mentioned (MC 106, 213).

2.18   We were also struck by the number of cases in which parents or parent figures asked for children to be removed in one way or another. Mrs Godfrey kept asking for a holiday for Lisa, or for a full-time nursery place, and would not be put off by offers of child guidance (LG 22, 45). On one occasion when she said she wanted Lisa taken away she also said she was striking her again (LG 41). Similar warnings were given to the general practitioner by Mr Auckland (JA 50) and to the health visitor by

Mrs Piazzani (MPI 19(f)) and Mrs Howlett (NH p.3, entry for 18.4.74). Richard Clark's private foster parents asked for the children to be removed, ostensibly because their father was not offering sufficient support. As their own children had previously been removed and then placed home again under supervision it must have been difficult for them to suggest they could not cope (RC 35). In the Lester Chapman case, Lester's stepfather twice called for help in relation to Wendy, the first time stating that she would have to go into care. On both occasions she was removed from home (LC 127, 133). Later, when Lester ran away for the second time, Mr Chapman "said that he did not want Lester in the house" (LC 188), although he did not demand immediate action, and later still he threatened to leave the boy on the social worker's doorstep in an effort to apply pressure for something to be done (LC 204). Part of this pressure stemmed from a genuine concern for the child's safety, and a search for a solution to the child's behaviour problems, rather than a wish to be permanently parted from him (LC 240).

2.19   Finally, the Maria Mehmedagi report makes the point that warnings of abuse should be taken seriously when voiced not only by parents or other members of the public, but also by other professionals. The second health visitor asked the general practitioner to see the child urgently because she suspected non-accidental injury but he declined to visit. The report comments: "Even though....he did not realise that Maria had already been injured on two occasions, we feel [the general practitioner] should have responded to the very real and justified concern expressed by the second health visitor....he should have recognised the health visitor as a professional colleague and should have responded to her call for support and assistance" (MM 39).

Assessment: A Continuing Process
2.20   Before action can be taken on a case there must be as full an assessment or diagnosis as circumstances permit. The inquiry reports devote a great deal of attention to this topic. They stress the need for assessment to be both complete and accurate. The reports also remind us, however, that the process of assessment and re-assessment must continue as the case develops, to ensure that the original plan of action remains appropriate, or is revised.

Complete and Accurate Information
2.21   The reports highlight a fundamental need for information to be as complete as possible. All immediately available data should be gathered,

and all potentially useful sources of further information should be identified and consulted. These include not only professional contacts but also
neighbours and relations, whom the reports show frequently to have held
useful information (see paragraph 2.48 et seq). The most common picture
to emerge from the reports is one of information scattered between a
number of agencies, and never systematically collated to form a more
complete view than individual workers could achieve separately. The
perspectives of doctor, social worker, health visitor or probation officer will
differ according to their skills, and the function of the agency in which they
work. In addition to these professions, the police, who have particular
responsibilities and skills in gathering information, and the legal profession
may also be involved. "The key failure", in the Steven Meurs case for
example, was the "lack of understanding of the overall situation which con-
fronted social worker, NSPCC, health visitor and family doctor and of
which each was only partly informed" (SMS 8.02). (Other references:
CT 41; PB 84; GB(1) 37; NH p.10, 6; MC 130; LG 188(d)).

2.22   The pooling of information is not to be seen as the purely passive
assembly of available facts from various quarters; it also requires actively
establishing and maintaining contacts. For example, a case worker with
experience in child care, says the Auckland report, "would have recognised
the need not only to liaise with the health visitor but also to turn to the
probation service, and to seek information about the mental health of
Mr John Auckland.... In our view an experienced case worker would also
have wanted to discuss the case with his predecessors" (JA 174). The same
report also notes a GP's failure to follow up comments by the DHSS
Regional Medical Officer, by contacting either the consultant psychiatrist,
health visiting service, or social services (JA 236). (Other reference: CT 26).

2.23   The reports also have much to say on accuracy of information. It is
self-evident that information, even if seemingly comprehensive, is useless,
and possibly dangerous, if inaccurate. There are many examples of errors in
the transmission of basic information. In the Karen Spencer case, the first
Case Conference was for some unidentified reason given incorrect information about her long and difficult birth and delayed discharge from
hospital. This resulted in a failure to be aware of a significant period of
separation from her mother, which, if known of, might have indicated the
need for further information about the mother's attitude to the child in
hospital (KS 2.18). The Darryn Clarke case was bedevilled by errors in the
transmission of information and the inquiry commented: "Some of the
problems are of a basic nature, for example the failure to check the spelling
of names and the accuracy of telephone numbers. We think the practice of

sending written confirmation of telephone communications should be
adopted in critical situations and where action is expected.... The practice
of delegating communication....inevitably carries with it the risk of
distortion" (DC 192). (Other reference: SMT 6.6).

2.24   Another frequent cause of inaccuracy is the failure to corroborate
information. Information obtained from clients, family and neighbours
may be particularly unreliable as they may have reasons for painting a rosier
picture than the facts may warrant. Karen Spencer's mother claimed
untruthfully to be visiting her child in hospital daily (KS 2.47); John
Auckland claimed that his daughter Marianne (whom he had battered to
death) died because he had a blackout and dropped her (JA 146) while his
wife said her death had been an accident (JA 148). The Lester Chapman
report warns against manipulation by clients, who "may seek to play off
one professional against another" (LC p.65 viii). (Other references:
NH p.11, 8; PB 131; MC 121, 123, 132).

2.25   Information, however complete, objective, unbiased and well
validated, is of value only if used. The GP in the Maria Colwell case had
been forewarned about the possibility of child abuse but examined the child
without reference to her medical card. The inquiry commented "one is at a
loss to know the purpose of such medical histories, if they are put out for a
doctor and not used by him" (MC 136).

(Other references: JA 176; RC 71; PB 84; MPE 3.50).

Psycho-social and Medical Assessment

2.26   The reports show that assessment requires more than just assembling
complete and accurate information. It also requires a disciplined, structured
approach by the individual professional workers responsible. The Maria
Colwell report points out the interconnection of physical health and social
and emotional background in children (MC 169) and there are examples of
failures by both social workers and doctors to carry out sufficiently comprehensive assessments or examinations. In the Malcolm Page case, for
instance, six different social workers were involved but "it is significant that
not one of them prepared an adequate assessment of the case covering the
family history, a diagnosis of the problems faced by the family and an
analysis of the alternatives for dealing with them" (MPE 5.33). There was
also no medical examination of the children, no assessment of Mrs Page's
health and state of mind, nor of Mr Page's role in the family (MPE 3.19).
In three cases (Malcolm Page, Maria Mehmedagi and Karen Spencer)
children were removed from home, committed to care by the courts, and

placed home on trial very soon afterwards without a full psycho-social assessment being made. In contrast, the Wayne Brewer inquiry found careful observation of minor injuries and prompt, thorough medical examination (WB 2.50, 2.51); recognition of the relevance of the parents' previous histories, as well as their current ability to cope in the face of multiple stresses (WB 2.23 et seq); and a careful distinction between material improvements to the home and problems of personality and relationship within the family (WB 2.37). (Other references: SP p.17, 4.8; MM 87, 141; KS 2.51, 2.88; PB 81, 84, 154; LG 188, 198).

2.27 The Malcolm Page report makes the clearest statements about psycho-social assessments. It indicates that they form the foundation of planning treatment, that the social worker is responsible for preparing them, and that the social worker's supervisor is responsible for seeing this is done (MPE 3.7). The report lists factors which should be included in the assessment:

"— the developmental history of the parents,
— the attitudes of the parents to each other and the children,
— the attitudes of the parents towards receiving help,
— the emotional needs of the children,
— the capability of the parents to meet the children's emotional and physical needs,
— the need for medical examination of the children or at least consultation with a general practitioner" (MPE 7.1).

The importance of preparing a social history report as part of the process is emphasised (MPE 7.2).

2.28   As well as pointing out the general importance of full medical assessments in child abuse cases, reports comment on their special value in certain circumstances. The Maria Colwell report criticised the failure to ensure that Maria was registered with a general practitioner when she returned to live with her mother, or even that she was medically examined: "these matters indicate either an insufficient awareness of the potential emotional dangers of the situation....on the part of the ....Social Services Department or a failure to arm themselves with the best sources of information to assess the development of that situation" (MC 79).

2.29   The Maria Colwell report also draws attention to the importance of medical assessment at crucial stages in a case, as a means of obtaining base line data for the measurement of subsequent change (MC 77). The Malcolm Page report re-iterates the point, and also discusses the importance of regularly monitoring a child's weight when abuse is suspected (MPE 5.23 et seq); the importance of seeing the child undressed (MPE 4.16); and a link between malnourishment and hypothermia in children (MPE 4.15). (Other references: SP p.20, 6.9; RC 71).

Appropriate Focus of Intervention

2.30   The advantage of a disciplined, structured approach to assessment is that it guards against focussing too narrowly, or on inappropriate matters. In many of the cases studied, for example, housing was mistakenly seen as the source of all difficulties. The Probation Officer in the Lisa Godfrey case felt "that the key to the Godreys' troubles was the housing situation" (LG 134). Despite a known history of bruising of which the Probation Officer had informed the SSD, and the fact that Mrs Godfrey was beginning to talk about battering her children, this Probation Officer's response, on being informed of further bruising, was to phone the Housing Department to hasten an application for rehousing (LG 38). When rehousing failed to solve the problems and the mother was asking for Lisa to be taken away, the Probation Officer "began to realise that the Godfreys' problems lay not only in housing, but in their personalities" (LG 135). (Other references: MPE 3.103; SP 5.1, 4.5; GB(1) 14)

2.31   Overemphasis on problems between other members of the family may distract attention from a child at risk. In the Neil Howlett case the main focus of concern was upon Neil's brother Stephen, who was seen as the scape-goat, whilst Neil was assumed to have a better relationship with his mother. "It is dangerous" warns the report "to pick up one factor and judge the risk in the situation by that alone" (NH p.15, 5(ii)). The report further recommended that if a case is to be taken to Court, "the proceedings should normally include full consideration of all children of the family" (NH p.16, 5 and 9). In the Karen Spencer case the inquiry noted that the Social Worker was focussing on the marital relationship. Although Karen had been committed to care because of abuse, the relationship between mother and child was "not seen as problematical" (KS 2.89, 2.92).

2.32   Perhaps the most difficult part of assessment is the interpretation of the information collected and the weighting of the various factors. The best illustration of this difficulty is probably the minority report on the Maria Colwell case. Much of this report deals with matters to which the social work member of the panel gave different weight from her colleagues, such as some items of information about events in the early years of Maria's life, and their meaning for Maria and her mother.

Continuous Re-assessment

2.33 The reports demonstrate that not only are situations constantly evolving and changing, but that new information becomes available reinforcing the need for continuing reassessment. The Malcolm Page report, for example, says "there were strong indications that the treatment plan was failing.....The signs were there....to read but they were not interpreted and did not lead to a critical examination of the treatment plan and of the options available" (MPE 3.63 et seq). Elsewhere the report also points out that it is necessary "to ensure that the management of the case is examined critically and that assumptions on which decisions are based are tested against the available information" (MPE 3.102). (Other references: LG 187; KS 2.77, 2.109, 2.110; NH p.16, 7).

2.34 The Malcolm Page report also refers to the importance of basing re-assessments on evidence collected over an adequate period of time: "'improvements' in the home conditions were noted [but]we consider that such 'improvements' were assessed over far too short a time scale......The family home help quarterly review was not a review at all; it was merely a statement of conditions on a particular date based on an assessment of the condition of one room" (MPE 3.100).

2.35 Continuous reassessment is particularly critical, even if particularly difficult, in long term cases where workers may have to analyse a wealth of material already available. In addition, these cases may involve many agencies, several departments within one agency, and numerous changes of worker. In the Stephen Menheniott case, for example, Stephen was in care most of his life and many departments were involved. The family was highly mobile, and indeed at one stage had a nomadic existence. Nine local authorities were at some time involved, and the members of the inquiry read thirteen files from various agencies, each of which "had something new to tell us" (SMT 4.2.1). The inquiry considered there was "no substitute for face to face discussion" in such a complex situation (SMT 4.2.3).

Intervention: Planning and Carrying out Treatment

2.36 A thorough assessment should lead to the formulation and implementation of a clear plan of action. Given the frequent references to the absence of comprehensive written assessments it is perhaps not surprising that the reports say relatively little about the relationship between assessments made and the ensuing action. The reports do, however, note certain dangers such as basing decisions on imcomplete information, making unclear decisions, and simply failing to implement them.

Planning

2.37 Several reports point out the need to formulate a plan, once the assessment has shown action to be necessary. The Malcolm Page report puts it most clearly: "It [is] essential for the management of cases of this kind to be based on a clear treatment plan which is constantly reviewed and kept up to date" (MPE 2.23). (Other references: WB 5.8; LG 175; CT 58, 125).

2.38 It is important to consider all alternatives when formulating a plan of action. The Richard Clark inquiry criticised the failure to consider any alternatives to leaving the boys with the Duncans, such as pressing the father to give up his evening job or offering him some form of financial assistance to enable him to do so. A day nursery place for Richard or the services of a home help might also have been considered (RC 66). (Other references: MPE 3.102; MM 61, 83).

2.39 The Karen Spencer report draws attention to uncertainties about the purpose of the plan adopted at one stage in the case. The clear lesson is that planning has no value if goals are not clearly defined, since the success or failure of the plan cannot otherwise be measured. It was arranged that the health visitor and social worker should pay weekend visits alternatively. This plan was not carried out and the report suggests that one reason may have been that no express purpose for these visits had been worked out and agreed: "What was the idea behind this....plan for weekend visits? In the Health Visitor's mind it was clearly to provide opportunities for teaching Mrs Spencer how better to manage her baby....This can only be done effectively when the child is there with the mother. I am not sure how far the Social Worker also saw a need to work upon the emotional relationship of mother and child; if he *did* see this as of great importance, the failure to act on the plan of visits is harder to explain" (KS 2.79). (Other reference: MM 100, 107).

2.40 The Auckland report, stressing the need for clarity of purpose rather than frequency of visiting, says: "We expressly refrain from criticising the overall frequency of [the social worker's] visits...because we are very conscious of the pressures on her at the material time, and in general we consider it more important that a proper order of priorities should be set out, and that what is done should be done well, than that objectives should be set which, with available resources, are clearly unattainable" (JA 152).

2.41 It is not always only the workers involved who need to be clear about the purpose of the intervention. A crucial failure in the Malcolm Page case, according to the report, was that workers did not make clear to the child's father what was expected of him: "the social workers should have made specific arrangements with Mr Page concerning their expectations and his willingness to provide appropriate bedding before allowing the children to return home. Where there is a need for both the workers in the case and the clients to be clear about the objectives to be achieved, these should be put into writing and a copy given to the clients" (MPE 3.51).

Decisions

2.42 It is worth repeating in the context of planning action that reports illustrate a fundamental need for decisions to be based on adequate information (see paragraph 2.21 et seq). Weekend leave arrangements in the Karen Spencer case were made when there were still gaps in the information about the family and the important implications of this decision especially in terms of the effect upon any future application for discharge of the order, led the inquiry to conclude that such a programme of home leave should never be instituted without full information (KS 2.62). (Other reference: MM 55).

2.43 The Maria Mehmedagi inquiry drew attention to the fact that decisions can be assumed that have never actually been made. A case conference was held to discuss Maria's future while she was in hospital. "The one vital decision, that Maria should be returned to her parents, seems to have been assumed without full discussion. The differences turned only on when and under what conditions she should return home" (MM 79). The Malcolm Page report also stresses the need for clear decisions. It says "the message is that the case conference should be clear in its statements and expectations about who had to do what with whom and when" (MPE 5.12). (Other references: JA 151; KS 2.110).

2.44 A number of reports also comment on the role of senior officers in decision making. The Maria Mehmedagi and Malcolm Page reports stress the need for senior officers to make sure that accurate assessments have been made and that staff understand what they must do (MM 61, 123; MPE 7.6). Other reports point out that it is dangerous for senior officers to make or endorse decisions on the basis of incomplete, often verbal, briefing (PB 93; RC 64, 79; DC 102, 103).

Implementation

2.45 Once a plan of action has been adopted and clear decisions taken, they must be implemented: there are several instances in the reports of decisions simply not being carried out. In the Karen Spencer case, immediate reactions to Karen's first injury are described as "swift and efficient". But at a later case conference it was agreed, among other things, that a psychiatric assessment of the mother should be arranged. The psychiatric referral was not made, and the omission was not recognised until the next case conference. Even then a letter of referral prepared by the GP was not sent. There was no indication in the minutes of the case conference as to who should have taken action (KS 2.60). (Other references: LC 101; MPI 19(e)).

2.46   A potentially dangerous situation can be caused when intervention becomes routine or "token", without a clear follow-through from plan to implementation. In the period after Susan Auckland returned home the social services, the health visiting service and the general practice all "seem to have operated at a low level". Over a period of three weeks immediately after her return the social services "made one visit to a convicted child-killer who had for the first time been left in sole charge of three small children.... No liaison was established between the social services and the health visiting service, and the latter service did not in fact visit at all". Finally, the general practitioner "was once again content to issue certificates stating that Mr Auckland was suffering from nervous debility in a way which suggests that, [in the GP's eyes], his patient was entitled at any time to receive such certificates for an unlimited period on demand" (JA 230). This "low level of activity" continued up to the time of the child's death some six weeks later (JA 244).

2.47   Finally, there are reminders that decisions made in critical situations should be implemented as a matter of urgency. In the Richard Clark case, after numerous expressions of concern from other workers and from family members, the social worker herself became worried that the child might be being battered and in consultation with her senior it was decided he should be removed. However, it was decided to postpone action until after a meeting with the childrens' father two days later. The inquiry considered "that once the need to remove Richard had been accepted this should have been done as soon as possible without waiting for the further two days which must inevitably elapse if removal was to be postponed until after the meeting with Mr Clark" (RC 72). In the event the matter was not considered again as Mr Clark did not keep the appointment and the next morning the social worker found Richard's condition had seriously deteriorated. She could not contact the health visitor but she called the GP shortly after mid-day and told the receptionist that the matter seemed "fairly urgent". She also told her Senior that Richard "needed urgent medical attention". Further phone calls were made to the GP who eventually saw Richard at 4.20 pm and arranged immediate admission to hospital. The inquiry concluded, with hindsight, that the social worker should have taken the decision to have the child removed to hospital immediately without waiting for the GP to visit (RC 73). (Other reference: CT 76).

Investigating Allegations of Abuse

2.48   Allegations of neglect or ill-treatment play such an important part in the reports that they merit separate consideration. Indeed the law makes special provision for dealing with complaints of neglect or ill-treatment by placing a responsibility on the local authority to cause enquiries to be made into any information received suggesting abuse (see paragraph 1.4 and Appendix 3). Although the basic processes of assessment and decision-making are the same in all situations requiring intervention, allegations of abuse need to be investigated with great urgency and it is apparent from the reports that this is an area of practice which presents difficulties.

2.49   It we include the expressions of concern by Karen Spencer's foster parents about the state of the child's buttocks (KS 2.148), then all but one of the cases contain one or more examples of allegations of neglect or ill-treatment from relatives, neighbours, playgroup leaders, members of the community who chose to remain anonymous or, in the case of Lester Chapman, from the child himself. In a number of cases—Maria Colwell, Lester Chapman, Carly Taylor, Darryn Clarke—there were numerous complaints. The exception is the Auckland case, where the inquiry commented on the failure of neighbours, who "must have realised what, on occasions, went on in the Auckland's household", to raise any alarm signals, and remarked that the extended family, blindly prejudiced in favour of Mr Auckland, were "virtually useless" as a protection for the children, although they were relied on (JA 19, 21). In most cases, however, neighbours or relatives *did* notice that things were not well and passed the information to one of the child protection agencies.

Evaluation of Complaints

2.50   Firstly there is the problem of deciding whether information—allegations or even rumours—is sufficiently serious and well founded to initiate enquiries. A number of reports contain examples of information (largely validated by subsequent events and by the inquiries) being discounted as "idle gossip", or "unreliable, inaccurate" or "exaggerated". In the Carly Taylor case persistent warnings to a Senior Social Worker met with a "bland and unconcerned response" (CT 69), and the mounting sense of crisis on the part of relatives and lay people was not shared by professionals (CT 78). (Other references: DC 148; MPI 22; SMS 8.09, 10.11, 12.06; MC 80, 96).

2.51   These problems are discussed in the Maria Colwell report, as are the practical difficulties of carrying out investigations without fanning the flames of local hostility or jeopardising relationships with the families concerned. The problem of being seen by complainants to take their expressions of concern seriously whilst not pre-judging the outcome of any investigation is also discussed (MC 199 – 204). The general lesson from all these examples is that all allegations warrant serious and immediate consideration.

Investigation—prompt and thorough

2.52   There are examples of prompt and effective attention being paid to allegations, and of good liaison and joint action between those concerned leading to removal of children from situations of risk (WB 2.48, 2.62; LC 23, 24, 26; SP p.8, 5.4). But there are also numerous examples of failures to investigate thoroughly or, in some instances, at all. Complaints to SSDs or NSPCC were lost or not investigated at all, at least as far as the inquiries could discover, there being no record or recollection of some complaints (PB 69, 73; MC 94, 103, 110, 124, 143; CT 23). In some instances, as in the Maria Colwell case, NSPCC officers failed to follow their agency's standing instructions to investigate all such cases, sometimes simply referring information on to the SSD, and in the Darryn Clarke case the SSD did not investigate (MC 124, 143; SMS 6.10; DC 98, 99). Complainants who rang to give information and left their names and addresses or numbers were not contacted to clarify what further information they might have (MC 94, 140). (Other references: NH p.5, entry for 30.9.74; SMS 6.10, 6.12).

2.53   Perhaps the most striking example of failure to investigate effectively is the case of Darryn Clarke. The report consists, almost in its entirety, of an account of relatives' attempts, over a three-week period, to invoke the help of one of the three agencies with child protection powers in finding Darryn and investigating their suspicions that he was being abused by the mother's cohabitee. Throughout the case there were errors in communication (DC 71), lost or incorrect messages and referrals which were not confirmed in writing (DC 76). The inquiry concluded that the "prime purpose of any system designed to deal with the problem of non-accidental injury to children must be to secure a prompt response and ensure the safety of the child" (DC 202). In its recommendations (1 – 4) it laid even greater emphasis on urgency, advocating that any allegation of abuse should be investigated "as soon as possible and, in any event, within 24 hours". The report suggests that the agency to whom the allegation is made should carry out the investigation. Not everyone would agree with this and in many areas this responsibility is given to one of the three child protection agencies: SSD, NSPCC, or police. (Other reference: MC 85).

2.54   The same report's first recommendation also states that the child involved must be seen by the investigating agency. The same lesson is suggested by the Richard Clark report, which records that the social worker did not see Richard at his foster mother's when investigating an allegation by his father, because the child was said to be "ill in bed". "Nevertheless, without even mentioning bruises or ascertaining whether they existed, she satisfied herself by prolonged discussion with [the foster parents] that [the foster mother] had not been ill-treating Richard" (RC 69).

2.55   The Maria Colwell report observes that urgent investigation is necessary not only to ensure the safety of the child, "but, equally important, because if drastic action and even criminal proceedings might become necessary, then it was vital that medical opinion be sought without delay before the evidence of the bruising and injured eye literally faded or disappeared" (MC 85). The same point is made in the Neil Howlett report (NH p.11, 9).

2.56   As well as an initial need for urgency, some cases illustrate the need for persistence. Maria Colwell's parents fended off the investigating officers with various statements that Maria was out, which were found to be false. With persistence on the part of the NSPCC the child was eventually seen and found to have bi-lateral facial bruising and a bloodshot eye. The inquiry felt that the explanation offered for these injuries was too readily accepted in view of the earlier "barrage of lies and prevarication". The report identifies a number of further steps that should have been taken: the officer should have sought a pretext to see the child on her own; should have probed the parents further about the accident; should have sought to persuade the mother that the child should be immediately examined—the danger of eye or head injuries providing sufficient reason; should have gone with Maria and her mother to brief the doctor fully on the circumstances and, if the mother refused should, in consultation with a Senior Officer and with the SSD, have considered an immediate Place of Safety Order (MC 90). (Other references: RC 69; SMS 7.16).

2.57   Persistence is especially called for where initial visits fail to gain access. This problem has already been mentioned in the context of the recognition of abuse (paragraph 2.11). Difficulty in gaining access loomed large in the Carly Taylor case, together with a lack of positive action and persistence in the pursuit of repeated allegations of ill-treatment (CT 69 – 71, 89 – 90, 93 – 95). The inquiry pointed out that failure to gain access in these circumstances is a strong indicator for positive action. A police superintendent in evidence referred to the fact that the police are always willing to help when other services cannot obtain access to houses where it is believed that there may be a child or children left on their own. The inquiry recommended that professionals should be instructed about the significance of "no access visits", especially where there are signs that a child may be in the house alone, and that these instructions should include advice to enlist the aid of the police in obtaining access. The police are, of course, the only agency who can execute a warrant to enter, by force if necessary, and search for a child (under S.40 of the Children and Young Persons Act, 1933).

Proof of ill-treatment
2.58 Following a call which alleged ill-treatment in the Maria Colwell case, this potential source of evidence was not followed up because the NSPC officer "had felt that as the injury was an old one any action based upon it was impossible". A "curious piece of reasoning", thought the inquiry, "based upon a belief that a place of safety order is more easily obtained with evidence of fresh injury" (MC 94). Further information and evidence might also have been sought from the police, who had been called to a domestic fracas at Maria's home the previous day when a neighbour revealed that she had reported the family to the NSPCC and the parents were heard to blame each other for hitting Maria. These accusations were in contradiction to the explanation given to the investigating officers for Maria's injuries. This important point, that proof of *ill-treatment* does not necessarily rest on proof of *injury,* also arises in relation to the "Police Station incident" in the Lester Chapman case. Here a police surgeon offered the opinion that the child's injuries were not severe enough to warrant Place of Safety action and he was therefore sent home. The inquiry considered, however, that there *was* sufficient evidence to constitute grounds for a Place of Safety Order and that it was highly likely that the social worker would have taken appropriate action if there had been no medical opinion (LC 183). The Wayne Brewer inquiry felt that physical injury should be recognised as part of a pattern of related circumstances and that local authorities should be more ready to produce to the courts evidence, based on the expert testimony of experienced social workers, of the likelihood of parents injuring a child in the future (WB 4.22 – 4.25).

Follow-up

2.59 The Maria Colwell report commented on the failure to follow up the initial investigation of one of the allegations made by a neighbour. The SSD social worker led her NSPCC colleague and a neighbour to believe that she would "ensure" the child was medically examined (MC 97) but this was not done. She merely advised the mother to take the child to the doctor. Nor could the inquiry find any evidence that she visited the following week as intended. At the time of these events the child was the subject of a Supervision Order and the inquiry felt that if tact and skill could not achieve the desired results, consideration should have been given to reporting back to the Court the parents' lack of co-operation (MC 99).

Co-ordination

2.60 Preceding paragraphs show that in a number of cases more than one of the three child protection agencies were involved in the investigation of complaints. There are examples of good liaison between SSD and NSPCC in responding to allegations (LC 26; WB 2.48), which is the area of work where duplication of function mainly occurs (see paragraph 1.46 et seq). However, the existence of more than one agency with power to intervene can, instead of increasing the protection available, lead to children falling through the net because each agency is relying on another (DC 97–98, LC 101; MC 186–191). The police were called in in the Colwell, Meurs and Howlett cases, because children were left unattended or because of domestic incidents. They also picked up Lester Chapman after he ran away. The information and evidence they thus acquired was passed on promptly to the SSD in some instances (SMS 7.04), but not in others (MC 92, 117). The Colwell inquiry suggested that the police should have informed the SSD "as a matter of routine" of circumstances where a breach of the peace had centred upon a little girl and where the NSPCC were known to be involved (MC 92). In the Colwell case too, the school was very concerned about Maria's attendance as well as her general welfare and an EWO, with admirable persistence and in the face of verbal abuse, paid numerous visits to the home, but not until a very late stage was the help or collaboration of any child protection agency sought. Similarly, in the Howlett case, where the NSPCC was investigating complaints from various sources and issued warnings to the family, a GP was called in by a baby-sitter and found Stephen locked in his room, looking very ill, not responding to stimuli and covered with faeces. No contact was made with any child protection agency and potential evidence was lost (NH p.5, entry for 30.9.74).

2.61 These few examples serve to demonstrate how opportunities to intervene in child abuse may be lost when information which supports or confirms allegations of ill-treatment or neglect is not gathered together in one single agency. The Graham Bagnall report stresses that "the interests of child protection require that local authorities' directors of social services (as the officers statutorily responsible for such investigations) should expect to receive any potentially relevant information at an early stage" (GB(1) 37). The Maria Colwell report says, perhaps more strongly, "social workers may reasonably expect that matters of concern about individual families or children will be passed on to them by [other] agencies whether or not they have already indicated their interest to them" (MC 152).

Communication

2.62 Every report reveals problems in some aspect of communication between individuals and agencies, which is not surprising in view of the sheer number involved in each case. The Maria Colwell inquiry emphasised the importance of communication: "What has clearly emerged, at least to us, is a failure of system compounded of several factors of which the greatest and most obvious must be that of the lack of, or ineffectiveness of, communication and liaison. A system should so far as possible be able to absorb individual errors and yet function adequately" (MC 240). A great many communication problems are caused by confusion over roles, which were considered in Section 1. The following paragraphs note only what inquiries have said about basic matters of good practice in communication.

2.63 The Steven Meurs report points out that good communication will only be achieved if individual workers see their work as being interrelated with the work of others. "Many authorities....are endeavouring to build up a first-line defence in health care by linking family practitioners with the community nursing team, ie health visitors, district nurses and midwives. These efforts have at times been hampered by the need to persuade established workers to alter their approach to their tasks and to work as a team rather than as individuals" (SMS 11.07). (Other references: SMS 8.02; MPI 23).

2.64 The Steven Meurs inquiry also stressed the importance of direct links in communication: "Information *must* be pooled and...there *must* be direct confrontation wherever possible between workers 'at the coal face'. We found a good and friendly attitude between members of the staff at the King's Lynn Social Services Office and good liaison with some of the related services but not enough person-to-person contact....Above all it is useless to have to go up the chain of command in one service and down in the other..." (SMS 8.06).

2.65   One problem of inter-agency communication is that key words and expressions mean different things to different people. Commenting on communications between the Suffolk and the Cambridgeshire health and local authorities, the Simon Peacock report says: "The procedure for dealing with non-accidental injury as laid down by all four Authorities was followed in most respects and there was a measure of initiative in the additional contacts by telephone and letter made by the officers in Suffolk and their counterparts in Cambridgeshire. However there is no commonly agreed definition of what constitutes "urgency" or "risk of non-accidental injury". There is therefore no common terminology. The Committee were particularly concerned at the confusion that arose through the use of the term "at risk" as something different from "at risk of non-accidental injury" (SP p.19, 6.3).

Recording

2.66   The reports demonstrate that efficiency in recording, transmitting, and storing information is an essential and integral part of professional practice. The Maria Colwell report stressed the need to keep accurate records, concluding "It will be apparent from the preceding narrative that certain inaccuracies and deficiencies in the recording of visits and telephone messages played a part in the tragedy" (MC 153) despite the fact that "it is fair to say that the overall standard of case recording and recording of telephone messages was high and such criticisms as we make should be taken in that context" (MC 155). The Lester Chapman inquiry had difficulty in evaluating some of the action taken, because of the absence of records. There were no social work records of important factors, for example the mother's change of mind about the adoption of Lester and his sister in 1970 (LC 35), or the breakdown of her first marriage and her relationship with her second husband (LC 44). After February 1971, there were no written records of visits, though during this period Lester and his sister were in care and the decision was made to allow them home on trial (LC 50). Other examples of inadequate recording were pointed out in the Family Practitioner service (CT 85; JA 141—143), the health visiting service (LC 85; LG 86, 193; CT 129(6); SP p.19, 6.1.5), hospital services (MM 34), Education Welfare (MC 161), schools (MC 115), SSDs (CT 129(6); KS 3.3; JA 263), and the probation service (CT 117).

2.67   But simply writing things down is not enough—what is recorded must preserve all relevant information in an unambiguous form. The Carly Taylor report recommends that all files should contain a complete running record with summaries at appropriate intervals (CT 129(6)), and the Neil

Howlett report emphasises the importance of systematic methods of recording (NH p.17, 10). As well as the simple noting of what has happened or been said, the Maria Colwell inquiry identified four matters which had struck them as relevant: firstly, the recording of actual dates of visits; secondly the distinction between fact and impression: "A minor example, the statement 'has gained weight' (as distinct from 'appearing to have done so') should not be made unless this is proven"; thirdly the importance of making clear the source of the information which was "sometimes....confused in recording": "it is important for those with whom the field social worker is in consultation to have the distinction clear"; fourthly, the recording in detail of alleged incidents of ill-treatment (MC 156 et seq). The Malcolm Page report, too, stresses the importance of separating fact and opinion. If the two are not recorded separately, it argues, then the standards on which the opinions are based may not be made explicit: "One way of reading statements about the condition of the house such as 'not too bad' is 'not too bad for the Pages'. Case workers should....state clearly what standards they are expecting" (MPE 3.112). (Other references: JA 263, 269; KS 3.3; PB 207).

2.68   As well as problems and failures in preparing reports and records, some inquiries also found mistakes in transmitting information. There were cases where the recording of telephone messages and verbal information was an influential factor since vital information was sometimes lost or mis-interpreted. There are many examples in the Darryn Clarke report: inform-ation passed through several hands, becoming distorted and inaccurate en route; telephone messages to the police did not reach the officer concerned; and the emergency duty social worker's report was not forwarded to the relevant District as it stood, because it was on the back of another report and there was no photocopier (DC 65, 66, 74). (Other references: JA 107; MC 171).

2.69   Other reports highlight problems of handover and transfer. This was particularly evident in the Simon Peacock case, in which the family did not receive the attention it deserved after it moved from Suffolk to Cambridgeshire. Though the Suffolk health visitor telephoned her opposite number in Cambridgeshire as well as completing the notification form, the Cambridgeshire health visitor did not receive the health visiting records and so did not appreciate the gravity of the case. The system of transfer did not appear to have been understood by the Cambridgeshire health visitor who was not aware that she had specifically to request the records. The urgency of the case was not conveyed by the notification form, which the inquiry report criticised as inadequately completed and in any case unsatisfactory as it was for all children generally considered to be at risk as well as those on the Child Abuse Register (SP p.19, 6.1.5, 6.1.6). Other references: PB 141; LC 119; NH p.11, 7(v); CT 84).

2.70   Information must also be accessible both to those normally dealing with a case and to others who may have to take over, because of sickness or holidays for example. This means that both the form in which it is recorded and the way in which it is stored must be clear and comprehensible. On the form of recording, the Auckland inquiry said of the GP's day books: "The names of patients, their diagnosis or complaint, and the treatment, if any, were recorded on a daily basis in the order in which the patients were seen. We have inspected these day books; they contain useful information about the health of the patients, but in the form in which they are completed (ie in a daily attendance order) they are of no value whatsoever in giving an ongoing picture of the state of health of any individual patient" (JA 142). For social workers involved in what may become long term child care cases, where changes of worker are likely, full, accurate but accessible recording is of the greatest importance. In the case of Stephen Menheniott, for example, in which nine local authorities were involved, the inquiry panel saw thirteen files, each with something to contribute to a picture of the family which none of the individual authorities with parental responsibilities had ever constructed. The report says "all the files read were bulky and it took a great deal of time to sort out the sequence of events. It can readily be under-stood how officers operating under pressure were not able to make full use of the information available. Moreover it had to be sought from a number of sources" (SMT 4.5.1). (Other reference: KS 3.7).

2.71   On problems of storing information, the Paul Brown report records instances of lost and mislaid files, and comments on the fact that the doctor examining Paul's brother did not have all the existing medical information to hand, because it was scattered in a number of places (PB 132). The Lester Chapman report also notes failure to link up separate items of information (LC 115) and failure to retrieve information (LC 124) because of faults in the systems of managing information. (Other references: JA 143, 256; LG 200).

2.72   Finally, there are examples of records which, though actually available, were not used. In the Auckland report, for example, a referral to social services was made after Mr Auckland's son John Roy had been admitted to hospital with burns, but the social worker failed to check for any file already existing in her Division on the Auckland family, and therefore did not know the full circumstances of the death of a previous child (JA 151). In the Lisa Godfrey case the general practitioner also saw Mrs Godfrey without reference to records (LG 97,100), and failure to read the case file led to serious errors in the Paul Brown case, such as the assumption by some senior staff that Paul's mother did not know the address of her children's foster parents (PB 103). Because of this assumption, they did not think that she could simply go and remove the children, although that is in fact what she did. (Other references: LG 116; MM 34; MC 136; DC 103).

2.73   There are also one or two examples of senior officers in SSDs endorsing decisions without reference to written records and with only a partial knowledge and understanding of what they were endorsing. A senior social worker in the Auckland case had a "system of regularly reading, discussing and initialling" the social worker's case notes, and this seemed to the inquiry "to be sound practice which should be widespread" (JA 115). (Other references: MPE 5.33(iii), RC 36. 64).

SECTION 3 The Context of Professional Practice

3.1 The beginning of Section 2 noted that the picture emerging from the reports was one not of single gross errors but of numerous minor failures and misjudgements compounded by adverse circumstantial factors (paragraph 2.2). The reports have much to say about these circumstantial factors, which include training and experience, supervision, staffing and recruitment, accommodation and administrative support and the impact of three major reorganisations. We have grouped these matters together because although they do not form part of professional practice itself, they all determine in one way or another the conditions of practice. It is in this sense that we described them as "circumstantial" in Section 2: they are beyond the control of professionals at the time that decisions about individual cases are taken, but not, of course, beyond all control.

3.2 These factors commonly entail questions of resources, and several reports suggest a relation between resources allocated and the level and quality of services provided. The Neil Howlett, Paul Brown and John George Auckland reports, in particular, speak of inadequate, overstretched resources in both health and social services. The Paul Brown report says that "the extent and effectiveness of the services rendered to the public by a Social Services Department are circumscribed by the amount of money made available to the Department by the Social Services Committee which receives its budgetary allocation from the Council as a whole. In its turn the Council is circumscribed by central government...For the last 5 years central government has kept local authority spending on a tight rein and is likely to do so in the years ahead. This financial stringency has imposed to [sic] great strain on local authorities and their Social Services Departments" (PB 18).

3.3 Some reports note that a particular resource problem arose out of the expansion of services, especially social services, during the 1970's when most of the cases occurred. This created high expectations of what could be achieved: as the Paul Brown report puts it, "areas of need became areas of demand" (PB 19). But the expansion occurred "without adequate regard being paid to local and national manpower resources" (JA 275) and "led to difficulties in determining priorities within the services bearing in mind the staff and the resources available" (MPI 18(e)). According to the Paul Brown report, increased public expenditure constraints from the mid-1970's exacerbated the situation (PB 19).

3.4   There are various comments on this in the reports. The Neil Howlett inquiry suggested that if the public wished to have more fully trained professionals, it was the public's responsibility to pay (NH p.12, 3). The Paul Brown inquiry pointed out that "at times of financial stringency...the Social Services Committee and the Director of Social Services and his senior management, working together, have an even greater responsibility than usual for ensuring the wise deployment of available resources. In such times the protection of life and the fulfilment of statutory duties must come first" (PB 26). The Steven Meurs (SMS 13.06) and Neil Howlett (NH p.13, 5) reports also comment on the need to make the best use of available resources, the latter recommending among other things, clear criteria for identifying children at risk of abuse, and a clear framework within which all workers can operate.

Training and Experience
3.5   From the earliest reports there is a wealth of comment on the qualifications and experience of workers involved, and more particularly on the special training needed for good professional practice in child abuse cases, yet the Maria Mehmedagi inquiry was still saying in 1981 "We were surprised to find how little training the people most closely involved in this case had received" (MM 145). The following paragraphs draw together comments on who needs training and when, and look at aspects which the reports suggest need special attention.

Basic Training
3.6   Much of what the reports say about training relates to in-service training, but the question of basic professional training arises in relation to social work, where practitioners are not yet all qualified. Not all the reports comment, but there are a number which provide information on the qualifications of particular workers involved with a case, or which record proportions of qualified staff available in Departments, Areas or Teams. This proportion was seen to affect cases both directly, by determining

whether a case could be allocated to a qualified worker, and indirectly, by determining the proportion of difficult cases which qualified members of staff might be required to carry.

3.7 In the Carly Taylor case, 45% of basic grade social workers were unqualified (CT 106) and in the Darryn Clarke case only half of the SSD's basic grade social workers dealing with individual and family problems were qualified and these were unevenly distributed between offices (DC 176). In the particular team involved only 1 out of 7 social workers was qualified (DC 180). In one of the area offices involved with the Paul Brown case only one out of 17 social workers was qualified (PB 47). The effects of reorganisations (see paragraph 3.42 et seq) on the levels of trained staff is illustrated in Appendix D of the Stephen Menheniott report, which shows that the proportion of professionally qualified field social workers in the Children's Department climbed from only 45% in 1966 to 77% just before the Seebohm reorganisation,* dropped to 50% just after this reorganisation and dropped even further to 33% in the new SSD set up by local government reorganisation in 1974. There are frequent instances where unqualified officers were responsible for cases at critical times. In the Auckland case, for example, the worker assigned to the family at the time of Susan's birth was both unqualified and newly appointed (JA 165, 174), and a request for Susan's discharge from care was handled by a social work assistant (JA 222). Attempts to improve the situation by making qualification a requirement can merely result in further problems. As the Lester Chapman inquiry found, recruitment of qualified staff in the area was difficult and the qualification requirements therefore simply led to staff shortages (LC 55). (Other references: SMS 6.01, 6.02, NH p.9, 1; PB 11, 37; LG 31, 130).

3.8 Whilst supporting the view that training should be given priority, some reports draw attention to the fact that releasing staff for professional training may affect manning levels. In the Karen Spencer case, 80% of permanent social work staff employed by the SSD were qualified, but unqualified and inexperienced workers were employed on a contract basis to replace staff away on training courses (KS 3.22). Such contract workers were included in the 'Duty' officer system to cover emergency work arising out of office hours and the one involved in a particular crisis in the case had only 6½ months' experience and was on duty for the first time (KS 2.164). (Other references: PB 59; MPE 2.19).

---

* See the Report of the Committee on Local Authority and Allied Personal Social Services. HMSO, 1968 Cmnd 3703

Experience
3.9   Many reports deem experience sufficiently important to draw specific attention to it. The Wayne Brewer report, for example, refers to under-manning in the area, almost 100% turnover in staff and a decline in the number of staff with two years' post-qualifying experience (WB 7.4); despite these difficulties, Wayne was continuously supervised by trained workers and at the time of his death the family were supported by a qualified senior practitioner with special experience in the child care field (WB 7.8). Unfortunately, supervision in the home turned out to be an inadequate safeguard, as the social workers foresaw.

3.10   Two reports refer to the fact that the health visitors involved were newly qualified or inexperienced (JA 172, 267; NH p.9, 1). In two other cases where probation officers were involved, one had just completed his probationary year and one had only a few months experience (CT 52; LG 130). There are numerous references to inexperience in social work (PB 11; JA 262; LC 67; NH p.12, 3; SMS 6.01; SMT App D; MM 59; MPE 2.28; MPI 18(d)), and many references to inexperience in the particular area of local authority child care and child abuse work (MC 26; PB 37; DC 179; JA 149; KS 2.168; MM 59; MPE 2.25, 2.31; LG 209, 181(d); RC 76, 78). There are also numerous references to lack of experience in child abuse or non-accidental injuries amongst health visitors (DC 208; KS 2.20; MM 130); general practitioners (PB 158; KS 2.20; LG 98; MC 137); consultant psychiatrist (KS 2.117); Clinic Medical Officer (LG 76); and the police (DC 166).

Appropriate Recipients of Post-qualifying and In-service Training
3.11   The reports' comments on training embrace all statutory and voluntary agencies, their fieldworkers and their supervising staff. The Lisa Godfrey inquiry said "There is a specific need both for the education and training of staff within services having responsibility towards children.... Staff to whom such training...should be directed are (a) those who are in direct contact with children and their parents and whose identification of possible non-accidental injury may be crucial; (b) those who are the recipients of information from other workers, other services or members of the public; and (c) supervisory staff who may have particular responsibility for ensuring not only that work performed by their own staff is of an appropriate and adequate standard but that agency and inter-agency responsibilities are fulfilled" (LG 214). (Other references: DC 164, 201, 208; NH p.15, 5(iii); KS 3.24; LC p.66, xii; WB 13.1; MPE 2.31; SMS 11.04, 14.03; SP p.21,7.6; CT 121).

3.12 One particular group of staff, identified by the Maria Colwell inquiry, may not immediately come to mind in the context of child abuse training. The report says "we would...emphasise that not only social workers and other professionals are involved in the recording of messages. Clerical staff are often crucial in the system. Their training and instructions, especially concerning telephone communications, are vital elements in the protection of children at risk; in this we would, of course, include doctors' receptionists" (MC 163). (Other reference: DC 228).

3.13 The Wayne Brewer inquiry also suggested training for magistrates. "We think that Courts ought to be more aware of the advances in knowledge of this subject which are no longer conjectural but demonstrable conclusions. We think this would help them in making difficult decisions about the likelihood of a parent in a case like this subsequently injuring a child...We hope that those who are responsible for conducting training courses for Magistrates may include this topic in future courses" (WB 4.25, 4.26).

3.14 As well as these specific groups, a particular need for training is identified in places where there is a high staff turnover. The Lisa Godfrey inquiry was concerned that "Particular attention should be given to education, training and the maintenance and continuity of vigilance and of safeguarding procedures in situations where frequent changes of key staff are endemic (for example, in hospital outpatients' and casualty departments or where part-time professional staff are employed—including session clinic doctors—whose work is not normally supervised and whose opportunities for updating professional knowledge may be limited)" (LG 215).

Appropriate Topics
3.15 The need for alertness and knowledge led inquiries to advocate training in very wide terms. However, reports also single out specific areas as worthy of attention. The Malcolm Page report suggests that training should be given on the chairing of case conferences (MPE 5.13) and on social work assessment (MPE 5.34); the Stephen Menheniott report notes that "the work of carrying out a local authority's statutory parental functions...calls for a high degree of specialist skill. We suggest that priority should be given in training programmes, both nationally and locally, to the reinforcement of this skill." (SMT 7.4). In addition there are comments on the need for training in child care legislation (PB 60), in good recording (MC 156, 162; NH p.17, 10), and in supervising and staff management techniques (MPI p.12). Two reports refer to the need for training on other agencies' functions (DC 233; MPI p.12).

3.16   Inquiries singled out several aspects of working with patients/clients themselves as needing particular attention in training. The most commonly mentioned was the ability to recognise and interpret the first signs of abuse (KS 3.23; MPI p.12; WB 13.3; NH p.17, 10). The Maria Colwell report suggests that training for social workers in dealing with allegations of neglect or ill-treatment could be profitably explored (MC 199—204). Lastly, the Carly Taylor report identifies special training needs in recognising the significance of "no access" visits (see paragraph 2.11) and of drug misuse (CT 129).

Training Arrangements

3.17   The reports tend to concentrate on identifying training needs, rather than specifying how they should be met. Such references as there are tend to favour multi-professional, in-service courses or seminars (LC p.66, xii; MM 145; DC 233; WB 13.6; CT 121). The Lester Chapman and Darryn Clarke reports specifically suggest that Area Review Committees should take the lead in organising training (DC 233; LC 218). In the Malcolm Page case the inquiry noted that the local authority and health authority had appointed a Joint Training Officer and considered this approach "imaginative" (MPE 5.34).

Procedural Instructions

3.18   Several reports mention the importance of clear written instructions on policy and procedure for all staff. The Lisa Godfrey report recommends that these should cover such matters as the steps to be taken in the event of suspicion of non-accidental injury; the flagging of case notes; the restrictions on staff permitted to carry responsibility; arrangements for the regular assessment and review by a senior member of staff of developments and the focus of work; requirements on the recording of all significant matters; and inter-agency agreements on responsibilities and roles (LG 220). (Other references: CT 120, 121; MPI p.12; GB(1) 34, 36).

Genericism and Specialisation in Social Work

3.19   There is relatively little material in the reports that relates to the generic/specialist debate about the training of social workers or to "generic" social work practice. However, a number of reports make the point that efficient practice in child care and protection demands a high level of specialised knowledge and skill as well as experience. One or two suggest that in post-Seebohm Departments, dealing with a wider range of types of cases, it might be more difficult for social workers to acquire this knowledge and skill (RC 91; MC 209; SMT 5.8). The Richard Clark inquiry suggested that more attention needed to be paid to matching tasks to the competence and experience of the worker and that whilst Departments were responsible for various branches of social work it did not follow that every social worker should be properly equipped to deal with every type of case. More satisfactory results might be achieved if at least some of the workers specialised (RC 91). The Maria Colwell report, stressing the importance of training in direct work with children, considered that since the Seebohm re-organisation, on average field level social workers inevitably had less experience than their predecessors in a Children's Department and thought that this subject might be receiving less attention in training than before (MC 209). As well as direct work with children, the complex legal framework, exercising statutory parental functions, and assessing the risk of injury and neglect are seen as presenting particular problems.

3.20 The Karen Spencer report points to the difficulties of specialisation in rural areas, where some cases would have to be handled as part of a generic caseload and some problems might be encountered too infrequently to permit workers to acquire expertise through experience. It suggests that specialists with knowledge and experience of the treatment and management of non-accidental injury could advise keyworkers and supervisors, share in the review of cases, and assist in developing training programmes (KS 3.63, 3.64). (Other reference: RC 91).

Supervision

3.21 Most of the reports have some comment on the importance of supervision and support for fieldworkers involved in the complex, stressful area of child abuse. Workers particularly mentioned are social workers and health visitors. There are numerous references to basic grade staff, sometimes inexperienced and out of their depth, being left to work without adequate support and supervision in Social Services Departments (PB 50; SMS 6.03, 10.11; LC 78; SMT 4.8.2; MM 61, 114; JA 191, 193) and in the health visiting service (JA 204; LG 191; MM 123). Staff shortages, post-reorganisation problems, and staff sickness all affected adversely the quality of supervision. In the Darryn Clarke and Carly Taylor cases, the senior social workers were carrying cases but without either supervision or consultation (DC 181; CT 126(1)), and the Carly Taylor inquiry also commented on the large number of staff supervised by the Nursing Officer: apart from the health visitor involved in the case, she was responsible for 15 other health visitors, 8 school nurses and 7 school nurse assistants (CT 111).

The Nursing Officer in the Malcolm Page case was supervising 39 whole and part-time staff (MPE 2.36). (Other references: NH p.17, 13; MPI p.12; MM 146).

Supervision of Social Workers

3.22 The functions of supervising officers in Social Services Departments are described in some detail in the Malcolm Page report, which sees them as including: responsibility for supporting the social worker and sharing in major decisions; ensuring that a treatment plan is drawn up based upon an initial assessment which is as complete as possible; taking an active role in the systematic review of cases of children at risk; ensuring that the social worker updates the treatment plan in the light of new information and changing circumstances; and helping the social worker to manage his or her total case load (MPE 2.26). The Auckland report suggests that the case file of a family where a child may be at risk should be read by a senior social worker at regular intervals. The senior social worker should then discuss the case with the social worker responsible and initial the file. On each occasion the social worker and senior social worker should be considering the problems and needs of the family, the work to be undertaken by the social worker, and the frequency of visits. If there is any cause for anxiety about the safety of the child, it is of paramount importance that they should consider the possibility of initiating care proceedings (JA 264). The Karen Spencer and Neil Howlett reports mention the importance of recording supervisory disussions dealing with children at risk (KS 2.110; NH p.12, 4).

3.23 The Stephen Menheniott inquiry pointed out that supervision is necessary not only for basic grade workers. Stephen Menheniott's social worker was consecutively the area children's officer, the senior social worker and team leader and was both qualified and experienced. The onus to consult on the case management rested with her although a senior officer was available. In the panel's opinion "the responsibility for carrying individual cases is so heavy that supervision needs to be built into the system, whatever the seniority of the officer. Supervision provides the opportunity for scrutiny of the issues involved and there is always room for another professional perception" (SMT 4.8.2).

3.24 For social workers on out-of-hours emergency duty the Lester Chapman inquiry stressed a special need for supervisory support since problems arising at such times were by definition emergencies and might require difficult decisions. The inquiry considered that it was not enough to give workers the option of consulting a senior colleague where child abuse was involved: this should be obligatory (LC p.67 (xv), 185). (Other reference: KS 2.165, 2.168).

Supervision of Health Visitors
3.25 As the Karen Spencer report says, "there is nothing like the same tradition of supervision amongst health visitors" as among social workers (KS 3.17). The Malcolm Page report quotes the Health Visitors' Association Memorandum on Health Visiting and Child Abuse, which says "...Health Visitors work as independent practitioners, accepting individual responsibility for selecting their own priorities and making their own decisions within the framework of duties indicated during their training or usually prescribed in outline by their employing authority" (MPE 2.37).

3.26 However, the Karen Spencer report also notes that the position has been affected by the establishment of Nursing Officer posts (KS 3.17), and both this report and the Auckland report mention arrangements for health visitors to report monthly to their Nursing Officers (KS 3.21; JA 271). The Auckland inquiry commented "the quality of a health visitor's service is likely to be improved if she has regular personal contact with her immediate superior and her colleagues, and is not left to operate entirely on her own" (JA 272). (Other references: LG 191; MM 141).

3.27 The Memorandum quoted in the Malcolm Page report also emphasises that health visiting has mainly a preventive and monitoring, rather than remedial, function (MPE 2.38). The Auckland report comments "a health visitor to whom a family with problems is assigned must be properly briefed in relation to that family. She must know the problem and what is expected of her....beyond the care she is expected to give to every young child" (JA 268).

Purposes of Supervision
3.28 Some of the points covered here and under "Methods" (paragraphs 3.34 – 3.36) have already been touched on in the preceding paragraphs, but it may be useful to draw together comments which seem to us to illustrate basic principles common to all types of supervision.

3.29 For the inexperienced worker, supervision merges with training and there are comments that supervisors of such staff must bear in mind the need not only to direct, but also to inform and guide. The degree to which a social worker may become personally involved with a family was touched upon by the inquiry into the death of Steven Meurs. The panel believed that the social worker had good potential but that she was "probably out of her depth" (when allocated this case she was not professionally qualified and had been on the staff for only three months). "Perhaps through seeking to identify too closely with [Steven's mother] she failed to attach enough importance to some pointers which should have put her more on her guard as to the developing situation..." (SMS 6.02). The report goes on to say "what [the social worker] needed was fairly close supervision and guidance but it seems that her undoubted potential led her immediate superiors to leave her too much on her own" (SMS 6.03). (Other references: KS 3.9; JA 174).

3.30 Reports refer to supervision increasing objectivity and critical analysis in the process of assessment. The Karen Spencer report says "the monitoring function of the supervisor remains important however experienced and highly qualified the worker. I take monitoring to involve not just an awareness of what the social worker is doing and of the general treatment plan, but also a willingness to probe his assumptions, to test that they are based on adequate and reliable data, and are mutually consistent" (KS 3.9). (Other references: SMT 4.8.2; LG 203).

3.31 There are also comments that supervisors should require, and contribute to, the continuous review of cases. During a crucial period in the Malcolm Page case there were strong indications that the treatment plan was proving ineffective. Mrs Page was not taking the children to the local clinic, the family home help was not satisfied with the way things were going and the bedrooms were in an unsatisfactory state—all pointers to the fact that Mrs Page was not able to cope. A full re-assessment of the case by a senior social worker was warranted but did not occur. "Instead the social worker was left with the burden of restating requirements to the Pages and trying to maintain the original treatment plan in spite of the strong signs that this was failing" (MPE 3.66). (Other references: KS 3.9; LC 84).

3.32 Another aim of supervision is to ensure that, alongside the proper management of individual cases, the work as a whole is efficiently organised. Each worker should be helped "to manage his or her total case load" (MPE 2.26) and there should be means of providing "a check on the correct implementation of procedures" (SMT 7.3).

3.33 Finally, reports draw attention to the responsibility of management for the proper training and deployment of staff and the best allocation of tasks. The Mehmedagi inquiry said "we cannot emphasise too strongly the duty of senior management to ensure that all those who are or may be involved in cases of child abuse should have the suitable qualities and temperament, together with appropriate training and experience to deal with such cases" (MM 133). (Other references: LG 209; NH p.17, 12).

Methods of Supervision
3.34   A number of reports emphasise the need for supervision to be an integral part of the overall system of working. Individual initiative, whilst being a desirable attribute in certain respects, has to be tempered by systems of accountability, especially where workers are members of agencies which are responsible for their actions. The Maria Colwell inquiry commented "certain local authorities and agencies in Maria's case cannot escape censure because they must accept responsibility for the errors and omissions of their workers; because they are responsible for their supervision" (MC 243). (Other references: RC 80, 87; SMT 4.8.2; CT 126 (1); LG 220(d)).

3.35   A feature of the systematic approach recommended by some reports is the need for regularity and follow-up in supervision: single or random actions are inadequate. This may apply at the most senior level: an assistant director in the Carly Taylor case wrote a memorandum to the senior social worker, instructing him, amongst other things, to place the child on the child abuse register, but the senior social worker took no action for over a week. The inquiry commented: "We were...somewhat surprised that having sent his memorandum, the assistant director...took no further action to find out whether his instructions had been complied with." (CT 77). (Other references: MM 146; JA 264).

3.36   The Maria Mehmedagi report, among others, distinguishes between supervision sought on a voluntary basis, which it regards as inadequate, and supervision as active participation by the supervisor. "The supervision of health visitors by senior nursing staff should be positive, ie regular sessions at which the case is discussed and advice given. It should be more than 'being available if required'" (MM 141 (e)). But the point is also made that positive supervision should not be meddlesome. Over critical analysis of a social worker's case management could, according to the Paul Brown inquiry, result in a lack of confidence by the social worker in his own judgement to such an extent that he may become unwilling to act or express his view for fear of being seen to make a mistake. The panel thought that this defensive attitude had not been helped by previous inquiries and they believed that it was the role of the elected members of Social Services Committees and the senior management of the Social Services Departments to show support for their staff doing a vital job and acknowledge the fact that tragedies do occur. "With confidence in themselves and the knowledge of this support behind them, social workers can perform their professional task better and their senior managers can play a more equal role in the business of running the local authority" (PB 169). (Other references: MM 146; MPE 2.26, 2.35; KS 3.8 et seq).

Staffing and Recruitment

3.37   There are many references in the reports to staff shortages and to staff carrying caseloads which were too heavy. As far as health visitors were concerned, the Simon Peacock inquiry quoted the 1956 Jameson Committee's recommended ratio of one health visitor per 4,300 population.* During the time she was supervising the care of Simon, however, one health visitor in the case covered 14,000 population, with approximately 900 children under five (SP p.21, 7.5). The health visitor in the Howlett case was also overloaded (NH p.7, 3). The Simon Peacock and Karen Spencer inquiries mentioned the problem of covering large geographical areas (SP p.21, 7.5; KS 2.21). Straightforward shortages are recorded in the Max Piazzani (MPI 18(d)) and Steven Meurs (SMS 11.10) reports and the latter notes that health visiting services were unevenly distributed: 1:11,000, 1:7,000, and 1:6,800 in three different areas.

3.38   Social workers faced similar problems. Reports record heavy case-loads (MC 26; CT 101; JA 275; SMS 10.01), unallocated cases (SMT App E), understaffed offices (CT 126; SMT App E; PB 50; SP p.20, 6.8; NH p.9, 1; MPE 2.19) and one case where the inquiry considered the establishment was inadequate (SMS 10.07).

3.39   Staff recruitment was also found to present problems in some areas (MPE 2.18; CT 106; SMS 11.04; MPE 2.18), and the overall effects of staffing problems receive attention in a number of reports. The Malcolm Page report suggests that staff under pressure develop a "siege mentality" (MPE 2.20) and other reports catalogue a whole series of adverse effects: lowered morale and increased turnover (PB 57), reduced liaison with other agencies (SMS 10.09), tendency to gloss over problems in casework (NH p.12, 3) and a tendency to concentrate only on the most difficult or pressing cases (LC 55).

3.40   Services were also frequently affected by the absence of staff on holiday or sick leave. In the Carly Taylor case the social worker and health visitor went on leave at the same time during a period which proved to be

---

* An Inquiry into Health Visiting: Report of a Working Party on the Field of Work, Training and Recruitment of Health Visitors. Ministry of Health, Department of Health for Scotland and Ministry of Education, 1956.

crucial (CT 82). Matters were also affected by the Area Director's long spell of sick leave, during which the senior social worker, who was handling the case himself, also shared the role of area director with the other senior social workers in the area (CT 102). The possibility of supervision of the case was therefore severely restricted. When Paul Brown's mother and her husband arrived at the foster parent's house to remove their children the social worker involved was off sick and the area officer was on leave. In the absence of a social worker the foster parents allowed Mrs Brown to leave with the children (PB 96). Similarly while John George Auckland's social worker was on leave the social work assistant was left with no clear advice and made the critical decision to return the three children to their father (JA 222). Sick leave may also have influenced events in the Max Piazzani case, in which there were long gaps in health visiting because the health visitor was on sick leave for two months and then left the service without being replaced (MPI 19(d)). Stephen Menheniott was allowed to return home against the recommendations of a case conference, in part because the social worker was on sick leave (SMT 4.9.1). The need for adequate cover and accessible records in these circumstances seems plain.

Accommodation and Administrative Support

3.41 Mention is also made of back-up facilities such as accommodation and administrative staff in some reports, particularly Paul Brown. In this case, poor accommodation was thought to have increased sick leave (PB 58), damaged staff development by rendering supervision difficult (PB 46) and increased staff turnover (PB 57). The inquiry also thought that a shortage of administrative staff wasted social workers as a resource, since they "should be occupied mainly with their clients" (PB 36). The report comments: "Adequate administrative back-up is not a luxury for social workers, it is a necessity" (PB 36) and "Adequate accommodation is the necessary tool of the social worker just as machinery is for the factory worker" (PB 38). (Other references: SMS 10.08; DC 74).

Reorganisations

3.42 Eight reports mention the effects of major structural reorganisations on services (JA, PB, SMT, NH, MPI, SMS, LC, MC). The reorganisations involved were:

i. 1971: Social Services Committees set up by County and County Borough Councils under the Local Authority Social Services Act 1970.

ii. 1974: Health Service reorganised under the National Health Service Reorganisation Act 1973.

iii. 1974: Local authorities reorganised under the Local Government Act 1972.

3.43   Many of the problems of supervision, staffing, accommodation, etc, discussed in earlier paragraphs of this section, were judged by the inquiries to have arisen out of reorganisations. But these problems have been considered separately because the reports make clear that they may occur at any time, and not just during major structural upheavals. Here we look at the inquiries' specific comments on the problems stemming from the reorganisations, although the extent to which they materially affected the outcome of individual cases is not always clear. The John Auckland inquiry was in little doubt: "The disruption, although well-known, is rarely emphasised, but in this case it almost certainly contributed to depriving a child of supervision and support that were literally vital" (JA 276). The Max Piazzani inquiry, on the other hand, thought the effects of reoganisation must "remain a matter of conjecture" (MPI 20(e)).

The 1971 Reorganisation
3.44   The Lester Chapman report notes that after reorganisation caseloads in the SSD were "substantially higher", which made proper allocation of cases difficult (LC 54). The reorganisation also led in some circumstances to reduced supervision and the disruption of monitoring systems: "the former Reading children's department was small and structured, with clear guidelines and a fairly comprehensive system of checking... In 1971 this standard of recording and supervision changed strikingly... We were told of the difficulties of supervising social workers, who now had greater freedom to make their own professional decisions" (LC 53). (Other references: MC 288; SMT 6.7).

3.45   As social work became less specialised there was also loss of expertise as those who had previous experience in particular fields were promoted to manage teams covering a wide range of work. Again, the Lester Chapman report: "social workers were asked to...work with groups with which they had had no previous experience... Many social workers were not clear about the legislation governing their statutory responsibilities towards client groups with which they were unfamiliar" (LC 52). This state of affairs was widespread throughout the country, according to the Max Piazzani report (MPI 18(d)). (Other references: JA 112; PB 29).

3.46   The Paul Brown report points out that it was not the intention of the Seebohm committee that individual social workers should work "generically", but rather that there would be generic teams. It says: "The Seebohm Committee recognised the need to retain specialist skills at headquarters and even at Area level and did not intend former specialists to abandon everything on reorganisation, taking on completely new types of work. Rather it was intended that existing skills would be carried over into the new Departments but a combination of a more rational approach to social work and the provision of increased resources would lead to the emergence of the generic social work team" (PB 29).

The 1974 Reorganisations

3.47 The reorganisations in 1974 again brought breaks in case management as well as repetition of the earlier problems of reduced supervision, caseloads which were too high, loss of expertise, and staff shortages. Discontinuity was brought about by staff moves and changes in accommodation. In the Neil Howlett case, for example, "the member of the Community Medical Team who was very concerned about the family would have arranged a [case] conference had she not moved to another post at that time in the course of reorganisation". (NH p.11, 6). (Other references: JA 192; PB 7, 30, 37, 68).

3.48 The Steven Meurs inquiry, discussing interprofessional communication, particularly between the health visitor and social worker, considered that "the 'unification' of the Health Service [in 1974] was achieved only at the cost of creating a fresh line of separation between workers in the community and this must be effectively bridged" (SMS 11.01).

3.49 The John George Auckland inquiry summed up the problems as follows: "This case illustrates the dangers of drastic reorganisation. Personnel in both the social services and in the health visiting service were moved in large numbers, so that continuity of contact was broken, except fortunately at field level, and staff shortages were created, perhaps by the need to fill senior posts in the new organisation. In one service valuable documents were mislaid, and in neither service was the staff above field level effectively established in a supervisory role by the time that Susan Auckland died. This meant that at a vital time the social worker...and the health visitor...were working on their own without adeqaute support. Both were junior and relatively inexperienced, and it seems to us that only a drastic reorganisation affecting both services could have left them so exposed" (JA 193).

SECTION 4 Summary

4.1 This study is an attempt to make available in an accessible and compact form the main findings of a succession of inquiries into individual cases of child abuse. It would not be appropriate to end with a set of recommendations since, as the Introduction made clear, the study is not intended as DHSS guidance on good practice. Nor is it intended as a Departmental response to the inquiries' recommendations. We therefore end simply by summarising the main points made by the reports.

4.2 *Agency Functions:*

—cases usually involve several professions and two or more agencies, but effective work is often hampered by ignorance, or misunderstanding, of respective functions. Fundamental to understanding these is knowledge of the main features of the relevant statutory provision. In particular, the police and NSPCC have powers to protect children, but only the local social services authority has a duty to do so, as well as to provide alternative forms of care. The local authority, through its SSD, therefore has a central function in child abuse cases.

—there are many occasions when health workers can provide expert diagnosis, monitoring, or advice. Paediatricians', health visitors' and GPs' special knowledge is sometimes critical to the full assessment of a case, and their involvement therefore crucial.

—all workers need agreed arrangements for exchanging information and, where there is an overlap of function or activity, a clear and common understanding of the extent and purpose of each individual's involvement in the case.

—case conferences offer an important means of co-ordinating action, but they need to be called at appropriate junctures, to involve everyone with a contribution to make, and to be specific about who is doing what and to what end. They can recommend courses of action, but cannot take over the responsibility of individual services for carrying out their designated functions.

—the safety of the child is paramount. All those involved, especially social workers, therefore need to be mindful of the possibility of legal proceedings, and the need to collect evidence. Professional roles, particularly the social workers', are sometimes ambiguous.

4.3 *Professional Practice:*

—the overall impression of practice given by the reports is one of much good work interspersed with numerous omissions, mistakes and misjudgements by different workers at different times. These failures can compound one another, producing a far more serious cumulative effect.

—workers who might encounter child abuse must have the special knowledge, skills and experience to be able to recognise when it is taking place, or is likely to take place.

—many allegations of abuse by members of the public turn out to be well-founded. Such allegations should always be taken seriously and investigated urgently. The child or children must be seen.

—a major characteristic of many cases is the failure to bring together all available information and to use it in a structured, objective way, by carrying out full psycho-social and medical assessments. These require continuous re-examination and revision. The need for health monitoring is important, particularly in cases of neglect.

—a common cause of inappropriate or inadequate intervention is the lack of a clearly formulated plan of action. Decisions should always be explicit and objectives specified.

—it is important to see that decisions are carried out and their effectiveness kept under review.

—effective communication and records are integral to good practice. Inadequate professional responses often stem from communicating and recording inaccurately or not at all, from failing actively to tap sources of information instead of "waiting to be told", and from recording information in ways which make it difficult to use or collate.

4.4 *The Context of Professional Practice:*

—several factors, such as training, supervision, and staffing, influence professional practice in individual cases, or affect the general level and quality of services. These factors typically raise problems of resource allocation and reports mention the need to establish clear priorities when resources are limited.

—cases can involve workers who are unqualified, untrained or inexperienced (sometimes all three). There is a clear need for special training on child abuse matters, and especially for in-service, multi-professional courses.

—poor practice may arise from inadequate supervision. Effective supervision is crucial to supporting and monitoring staff, ensuring the regular and objective review of cases, and securing the best deployment of available resources and staff.

—staff shortages and poor facilities are mentioned frequently. The reports found these to be associated with low morale, high turnover, and laxer standards of work.

—major reorganisations in 1971 and 1974 were said to have caused over-stretched and dislocated services in several cases, although this did not necessarily mean that they had adversely affected their outcome.

APPENDIX 1 Background Information on the Inquiries and Reports

18 reports were included in the study. Information is grouped according to the type of inquiry, and arranged alphabetically within each section. The figures in brackets denote order of publication.

Secretary of State Inquiries

AUCKLAND John George (6)

Set up by: Secretary of State for Social Services

Membership: *Chairman* P J M Kennedy QC
Miss W Frost OBE SRN SCM HV QN
M N Hall MRCS LRCP
Miss P M Ride MA

Terms of reference:

"...to inquire into and report upon the provision and co-ordination of services to the family of John George Auckland by the relevant local authorities and health services and by any other persons or agencies..."

Title of report:

Report of the Committee of Inquiry into the provision and co-ordination of services to the family of John George Auckland.

Published: September 1975

Available from: HMSO

BROWN Paul (16)

Set up by: Secretary of State for Social Services

Membership: *Chairman* M Morland QC
Dr P Barbor: Consultant Paediatrician, Nottingham University Hospital
Dr Clifton: DSS, Bedfordshire
Miss A Salvin: AN(CH) Sheffield AHA(T)

Terms of reference: "to inquire into:

a. What information or professional opinion relating to Paul and Liam Brown existed, was made available to, or could have been obtained by, the relevant authorities;

b. The action taken by any relevant authority or by any individual in connection with such information or professional opinion;

c. The arrangements for communication within and between the relevant authorities and other persons and agencies holding information about Paul and Liam Brown;

d. The working relationships of the Social Services Committee within the Metropolitan Borough Council of the Wirral in so far as they are relevant to the discharge of functions of that Committee in relation to children.

and to report".

Title of report:

The Report of the Committee of Inquiry into the case of Paul Steven Brown

Published: December 1980

Available from: HMSO (Cmnd 8107)

CLARK Richard (4)

Set up by: Secretary of State for Scotland

Membership: *Chairman* C E Jauncey QC
                       Dr D M Douglas MD FRCP FRCPE DCH
                       Miss M Browne BA AASPW OBE

Terms of reference:

"...to enquire into and report on the consideration given and steps taken towards securing the welfare of Richard Clark by Perth Town Council and other bodies or persons concerned."

Title of report:

Report of the Committee of Inquiry into the Consideration given and steps taken towards securing the welfare of Richard Clark by Perth Town Council and other bodies or persons concerned.

Published: January 1975

Available from: HMSO

CLARKE Darryn (14)

Set up by: Secretary of State for Social Services

Membership: *Chairman* J Hugill QC
J Chant, DSS, Somerset
Professor D Hull, Professor of Child Health, Nottingham University
Miss M E Lindars OBE, ANO Bucks AHA

Terms of reference: "...to enquire into:

a. the information about Darryn Clarke and his family that was made available to the relevant. authorities, or could have been obtained by them, during the period preceding his death;

b. the responses by the authorities to that information, including the professional decisions made;

c. the arrangements for communication within and between the relevant authorities and between them and other persons and agencies holding information about Darryn Clarke and his family."

Title of report:

Report of the Committee of Inquiry into the Actions of the Authorities and Agencies relating to Darryn James Clarke.

Published: November 1979

Available from: HMSO (Cmnd 7730)

COLWELL Maria (2)

Set up by: Secretary of State for Social Services

Membership: *Chairman:* T G Field-Fisher QC TD MA
Alderman Mrs M R Davey
Miss O Stevenson MA

Terms of reference:

"...to inquire into and report upon the care and supervision provided by local authorities and other agencies in relation to Maria Colwell and the co-ordination between them."

Title of report:

Report of the Committee of Inquiry into the Care and Supervision Provided in Relation to Maria Colwell.

Published: April 1974

Available from: HMSO

DHSS Inquiry

MENHENIOTT Stephen (12)

Set up by:	Department of Health and Social Security
Membership:	Miss C Jayne, PSWSO, DHSS
	Miss J Acton, SWSO, DHSS
	J Wheatley, SWSO, DHSS

Terms of reference:

"1. To examine the decision by East Sussex authorities in 1972 to allow Stephen Menheniott to live with his father in the Isles of Scilly and the subsequent exercise of their parental rights and powers and the level of supervision afforded.

2. To consider whether subsequent changes made in the policies, procedures and practice then in operation in East Sussex have made good any shortcomings revealed by this examination.

3. To indicate whether there are any general lessons that can be derived from this case and

4. To prepare a report for publication."

Title of report:

Report of the Social Work Service of DHSS into certain aspects of the management of the case of Stephen Menheniott.

Published: September 1978

Available from: HMSO

Local Inquiries

BAGNALL Graham (1)

1. Set up by: Salop County Council

   Membership: *Chairman* A C Williams, Chairman, Social Services Committee, Salop CC
   A P Sykes, Chairman, Salop CC
   G R Fletcher, Vice-Chairman, Salop CC
   Dr B E Marsh, Vice-Chairman, Social Services Committee
   A W Gurden, Member of Social Services Committee
   Observer: Miss J Acton, SWSO, DHSS

Terms of reference

"...to examine the circumstances surrounding the death of Graham Bagnall and to consider the specific and general issues which arose from it in relation to the working of the Council's Departments and their relationship with outside bodies concerned with child protection..."

Title of report:

Report of Working Party of Social Services Committee. Inquiry into the circumstances surrounding the death of Graham Bagnall and the role of the County Council's Social Services.

Published: January 1973

Available from: Shropshire County Council, The Shirehall, Abbey Foregate, Shrewsbury SY2 6ND

2. Set up by: Shrewsbury Group Hospital Management Committee

Membership: *Chairman* F W Leath, Chairman, HMC
Cllr Mrs L I Butler, Member, HMC
Mrs E Harrison, Member, HMC
Mrs F F Houghton, Member, HMC
Mrs O D Wakeman, Member, HMC
E J Whitfield, Member, HMC
Dr E G Rees, Vice-Chairman, Group Medical Executive Committee

Terms of reference:

"To enquire into the circumstances leading up to the death of Graham Bagnall insofar as the Hospital Authority were concerned, with particular reference to the Report on this matter produced by a Working Party of the Social Services Committee of the Salop County Council".

Title of report:

Report of the Committee of Enquiry of the Hospital Management Committee into the circumstances leading up to the death of Graham Bagnall insofar as the Hospital Authority were concerned.

Published: March 1973

BREWER Wayne (9)

Set up by: Somerset Area Review Committee

Membership: *Chairman* D J R Clark, Second Deputy Chief Executive and Dep County Solicitor, Somerset CC

Dr S Henderson JP, General Practitioner, Somerset Local Medical Committee

Miss M K J Stephens, AN(CH and LA Liaison), Somerset AHA

D H Stanley, AD (Field & Domiciliary Services), Somerset CC SSD

Terms of reference:

"a. to review the guidelines which the Committee have designed for those professionally concerned with children considered to be at risk of non-accidental injury; and

b. to achieve constructively the agencies concerned of any change in practice indicated or any general lessons to be learned."

Title of report:

Wayne Brewer. Report of the Review Panel

Published: March 1977

Available from: Somerset Area Review Committee for non-accidental injury to children, County Hall, Taunton, Somerset TA1 4DY Tel: 0823 3451.

CHAPMAN Lester (13)

Set up by: Berkshire and Hampshire County Councils and Area Health Authorities

Membership: *Chairman* John Hall QC

F Buckwell JP, City of Oxford

Mrs F Gray, AN(CH/LA Liaison), Herts AHA

Dr A Jackson, Consultant Paediatrician, The London Hospital and the Queen Elizabeth Hospital for Children

Miss R Pugh Thomas, SWSO, DHSS

Terms of reference:

"To inquire into the circumstances surrounding Lester Chapman's death and to review the discharge by the four authorities of their functions in respect of his protection and the provision of care and services to him and his family".

Title of report:

Lester Chapman Inquiry Report

Published: October 1979

Available from: Archives Office, Shire Hall, Reading, Berkshire.

GODFREY Lisa (5)

Set up by: Lambeth, Southwark and Lewisham AHA(T), Inner London Probation and After Care Committee, London Borough of Lambeth

Membership: *Chairman* R Lascelles MBE
Miss J B Rule MA SRN RNT, Lambeth, Southwark & Lewisham AHA(T)
Mrs H A Halpin JP, Inner London Probation and After Care Committee
Councillor Mrs R Verden, London Borough of Lambeth
Assessors: Mr R W Spiers (HO)
Miss J H Acton (DHSS)

Terms of reference:

"...to inquire into and report upon the co-ordination of services for the prevention and management of cases of non-accidental injury to children and in particular the lessons to be learned from the case of Lisa Godfrey."

Title of report:

Report of the Joint Committee of Inquiry into Non-accidental Injury to Children, with particular reference to the case of Lisa Godfrey.

Published: 1975

Available from: Lambeth Social Services Department, Blue Star House, 234 – 244 Stockwell Road, London SW9 9SR Tel: 01 – 274 7722.

HOWLETT Neil (8)

Set up by: City of Birmingham District Council, Birmingham AHA

Membership: *Chairman:* F A Allen, Barrister-at-Law
                Miss J R Wilkes, Headmistress, King Edward VI High
                School for Girls, Birmingham
                Miss S Beer, SSW (Team Leader) Wandsworth SSD
                Miss M Woodier, Prof. Adviser, W Midlands
                Children's Regional Planning Committee
                Dr J Dawkins, Community Physician (Social Services)
                Northampton AHA
                Miss A Lamb, AN(CH) Dudley AHA

Terms of reference:

"...to enquire into the provision and co-ordination of services by,
and the liaison between the relevant local authorities and health
services and any other persons or agencies in respect of non-
accidental injury to children in the light of the death of Neil Howlett,
and to report."

Title of report:

Joint Inquiry arising from the death of Neil Howlett.

Published: November 1976

Available from: Birmingham DC Social Services Department, Snow
                  Hill House, PO Box 93, 10 – 15 Livery Street,
                  Birmingham B2 2PE. Tel: 021 235 9944

MEHMEDAGI Maria (18)

Set up by: London Borough of Southwark, Lambeth, Southwark
                and Lewisham AHA(T), Inner London Probation and
                After-Care Service

Membership: *Chairman* B H Wilson CBE MA LLB former Chief
                Executive LB Camden
                Dr A J Cash, Specialist in Community Medicine (Child
                Health), Warks AHA
                Mrs A Poole SRN SCM HV, ANO Surrey AHA
                Miss M Mason JP MA DMA, DSS Bolton MBC
                D Finch, Deputy Chief Probation Officer, Greater
                Manchester Probation and After-Care Service
                Observer: D Tomlinson, SWSO, DHSS

Terms of reference:

"to inquire into and report on the facts regarding the care and
services provided by the relevant authorities and the communications

between and within those authorities in the case of Maria Mehmedagi and her family''.

Title of report:

Maria Mehmedagi—Report of an Independent Inquiry

Published: June 1981

Available from: PR Dept, Town Hall, Peckham Road, London SE5

MEURS Steven (7)

Set up by: Norfolk County Council and Area Health Authority

Membership: *Chairman:* G C Godber CBE DL Former Chief Executive W Sussex CC
Mrs N M E Eady, Vice-Chairman of Social Services Committee of ACC, Councillor for Leicestershire CC
Dr S T G Gray, Former County Medical Officer of Health East Suffolk
F J B Long OBE, Former DSS, Hampshire CC
Miss G M Pittom ANO, Redbridge & Waltham AHA

Terms of reference:

"...to enquire into and report upon the provision and co-ordination of services to the family of Steven Meurs by the relevant local authorities and health service, and by other persons or agencies."

Title of report:

Report of the Review Body appointed to inquire into the death of Steven Meurs.

Published: December 1975

Available from: Norfolk Social Services Department, County Hall, Martineau Lane, Norwich NR1 2DH Tel: 0603 611122.

PAGE Malcolm (17)

Set up by: Essex County Council and Area Health Authority

Membership: *Chairman* Dr A Denham GP
J Pickett, NSPCC
K G Hall, Dep DSS, Essex CC
Mrs M Lawrie DNO, Essex AHA
Observer: Miss R Pugh Thomas, SWSO, DHSS

Terms of reference:

"To consider the case of the child Malcolm Page and to indicate whether there are any lessons that can be learned from this case and to report".

Title of report:

Malcolm Page: Report by the Panel appointed by the Essex ARC

Published: March 1981

Available from: Essex County Council, County Hall, Chelmsford, Essex CM1 1LX

PEACOCK Simon (10)

Set up by: Cambridgeshire and Suffolk County Councils and Area Health Authorities

Membership: *Chairman* A Lamb CBE JP, Chairman of Juvenile Bench for City of Derby, formerly Chairman of Derbyshire AHA
Miss M Hartnoll BA, Director of Social Work, Grampian Regional Council, formerly Divisional Director of Social Services, Berks CC
Mrs B Willis RGN SCM HV QN, AN(CH) Devon AHA

Terms of reference:

"1.   To enquire into the services made available to the Peacock family.

2.   To enquire into the arrangements for communications between the Authorities concerned in this particular case.

3.   To submit a report for publication: the final form of any document to be published to be decided by the Committee of Enquiry."

Title of report:

Report of Committee of Enquiry concerning Simon Peacock

Published: January 1978

Available from: Cambridgeshire Social Services Department, Castle Court, Castle Hill, Shire Hall, Cambridge CB3 0AP.

PIAZZANI Max (3)

Set up by: Essex County Council and Area Health Authority

Membership: *Chairman* A Davies CBE DL, Former Clerk of Nottinghamshire CC

M Hamilton MD FRCP
Sir John Hanbury CBE
MA FPS FRIC   } Members of Essex AHA
D R Millard

Councillor S G Barnett
FBIM   Members of Essex CC
Councillor A Jones MBE
JP DL
Mrs J C Martin

Observer: Miss E White RRC TD SRN SCM, Principal Nursing Officer, DHSS

Terms of reference:

"To enquire into and report (to the County Council and the Area Health Authority) upon the co-ordination of the services for the prevention, and management of cases, of non-accidental injury to children and in particular to consider what lessons can be learnt from the case of the child Max Piazzani who died in Basildon Hospital on 4 August 1973".

Title of report:

Report of the Joint Committee set up to consider co-ordination of services concerned with non-accidental injury to children

Published: September 1974

Available from: Essex County Council Social Services Department, Kensal House, 77 Springfield Road, Chelmsford, Essex CM2 6JC Tel: 0245 67181

SPENCER Karen (11)

Set up by: Derbyshire County Council and Area Health Authority

Membership: Professor J D McLean, Professor of Law in Sheffield University.

Assessors

Miss M Addy, AN(CH) Derbyshire AHA

Dr J A Beal, Specialist in Community Medicine (Child Health) Derbyshire AHA

P F Bye, Deputy DSS, Derbyshire CC
J Pickett, Regional Social Work Manager, NSPCC, Manchester
Professor S Brandon, Professor of Psychiatry in the University of Leicester
Observer: F T Woodley, DHSS

Terms of reference:

"to consider the circumstances leading up to the death of Karen Spencer and to recommend any necessary measures to improve the procedures in such cases".

Title of report:

Karen Spencer. Report by Professor J D McClean, Professor of Law in the University of Sheffield

Published: April 1978

Available from: Derbyshire Social Services Department, County Offices, Matlock, Derbyshire, DEH 3AC Tel: 0629 3411.

TAYLOR Carly (15)

Set up by: Leicestershire County Council and Area Health Authority (Teaching)

Membership: R E Millard CBE LLB JP, formerly Clerk of the Bucks CC
Dr A M Jepson MB BS FFCM, Area Specialist in Community Medicine (Child Health), Kensington, Chelsea & Westminster AHA(T)
D H Peterken, Deputy Chief Probation Officer, W Midlands County Probation and After-Care Service
G M Pittom SRN HV DN Cert, ANO Redbridge & Waltham Forest AHA
J Woodley MA (Cantab), Dip Ap Soc Studies, Dep DSS, Cambridgeshire CC
Observer: G Corsellis, AAPSW, SWSO, DHSS

Terms of reference:

"To inquire into the provision and co-ordination of services to the family of Carly Taylor by the relevant local authorities and health services and by other persons or agencies, and to report".

Title of report:

   Carly Taylor. Report of an Independent Inquiry.

Published: February 1980

Available from: Senior Assistant County Secretary, Leicestershire County Council, County Hall, Glenfield, Leicester LC3 8RA.

APPENDIX 2 Table of Workers and Others Involved in the Cases

Cases

Workers & others involved	J G Auckland	G Bagnall	W Brewer	P Brown	L Chapman	R Clark	D Clarke	M Colwell	L Godfrey	N Howlett	M Mehmedagi	S Menheniott	S Meurs	M Page	S Peacock	M Piazzani	K Spencer	C Taylor
Social Worker	●	●	●	●	●	●	●	●	●	●	●	●	●	●	●	●		●
Police	●			●	●	●	●	●	●	●		●	●	●		●		
Police Surgeon				●														
NSPCC/RSSPCC		●	●	●	●	●	●		●			●						
GP	●	●	●	●	●	●	●	●	●	●		●	●	●	●	●		●
Health Visitor	●	●	●	●	●		●	●	●	●		●	●	●	●	●		●
Paediatrician	●	●								●	●			●	●	●		●
Psychiatrist	●				●											●		
Accident & Emergency Dept											●			●				
Nurse		●		●				●	●	●								
School Nurse					●													
Dentist				●														
DHSS Regional Medical Officer											●							

Cases

	C Taylor	K Spencer	M Piazzani	S Peacock	M Page	S Meurs	S Menheniott	M Mehmedagi	N Howlett	L Godfrey	M Colwell	D Clarke	R Clark	L Chapman	P Brown	W Brewer	G Bagnall	J G Auckland
Day Nursery Staff	●					●					●						●	
Teacher	●						●	●				●			●			
Childminder																		
Education Welfare Officer						●						●			●			
Educational Psychologist															●			
Probation Officer	●					●	●		●		●			●				●
Housing Welfare Officer				●							●							
Homeless Persons Officer	●																	
Social Security Officer	●					●										●		●
Home Help																		
Vol. Worker																●	●	●
Magistrate		●				●	●		●	●		●	●			●	●	●
Family	●						●		●	●		●	●	●	●	●	●	
Foster Parents		●		●		●						●		●	●	●	●	
Neighbours	●						●			●		●	●					

APPENDIX 3 Main Legal Provisions

1　Child care legislation is extensive and complex. This appendix deals only with the bare bones essential to an understanding of what the reports say, particularly about agency functions (Section 1). Although many of the reports themselves quote and discuss the statutory provisions governing child care and protection, this appendix refers directly to the relevant Acts, for the sake of both brevity and clarity. It is not, however, to be read as an authoritative statement of the law. All references are to provisions as amended by subsequent legislation unless otherwise stated, and do not generally include provisions relating to the commission of offences by children or young persons, since these are not relevant to the present study.

Investigation
2　Section 2 of the Children and Young Persons Act 1969 states:

"2.—(1) If a local authority receive information suggesting that there are grounds for bringing care proceedings in respect of a child or young person who resides or is found in their area, it shall be the duty of the authority to cause enquiries to be made into the case unless they are satisfied that such enquiries are unnecessary.

(2) If it appears to a local authority that there are grounds for bringing care proceedings in respect of a child or young person who resides or is found in their area, it shall be the duty of the authority to exercise their power under the preceding section to bring care proceedings in respect of him unless they are satisfied that it is neither in his interest nor the public interest to do so or that some other person is about to do so or to charge him with an offence."

Thus the local authority, through its Social Services Committee*, is the main agency charged with the *duty* (as opposed to a *power*) of ensuring that

---

* We are referring here only to those parts of the Act relating to care and protection and not those dealing with truancy or delinquency. See the Home Office "Guide for Courts and Practitioners", paras 86 – 91.

any information suggesting a child in their area may need the protection of care proceedings is investigated. If it then appears that there are grounds for proceedings the local authority must bring such proceedings unless they are satisfied on the points specified above. In practice, many authorities lay down that where an allegation of neglect or ill-treatment is received it should be investigated "immediately" or "within 24 hours". Other persons who may bring care proceedings are the police or the NSPCC, both agencies having the power but not a duty to do so.

3   There are no powers of entry under the provisions of the C&YP Act 1969, but Section 40(1) of the C&YP Act 1933 (as amended by the C&YP Act 1963, Section 64 and Schedule 3(2)) provides that a justice of the peace may issue a warrant for the police either to remove a child to a place of safety, with or without a search, or to search for a child and remove it to a place of safety, if it is found to have been abused. Section 40(1) states:

"If it appears to a justice of the peace on information on oath laid by any person who, in the opinion of the justice, is acting in the interests of a child or young person, that there is reasonable cause to suspect—

a. that the child or young person has been or is being assaulted, ill-treated, or neglected in any place within the jurisdiction of the justice, in a manner likely to cause him unnecessary suffering, or injury to health; or

b. that any offence mentioned in the First Schedule to this Act has been or is being committed in respect of the child or young person,

the justice may issue a warrant authorising any constable named therein to search for the child or young person, and, if it is found that he has been or is being assaulted, ill-treated, or neglected in manner aforesaid, or that any such offence as aforesaid has been or is being committed in respect of him, to take him to a place of safety, or authorising any constable to remove him with or without search to a place of safety, and a child or young person taken to a place of safety in pursuance of such a warrant may be detained there until he can be brought before a juvenile court."

Section 40(3) sets out the scope of action the police are authorised to take: "Any constable authorised by warrant under this section to search for any child or young person, or to remove any child or young person with or without search, may enter (if need be by force) any house, building, or other place specified in the warrant, and may remove him therefrom".

Place of Safety Orders

4   Under Section 28(1) of the C&YP Act 1969 a child or young person may be removed to a place of safety for not more than 28 days on application *by any person* to a justice. The justice must be satisfied that the applicant has reasonable cause to believe either that any of the primary grounds set out in Section 1(2)(a) to (e) for care proceedings is satisfied or that an appropriate court would find the condition set out in Section 1(2)(b) satisfied (see para 7). Under Section 28(2) the police may detain a child or young person for not more than 8 days on similar grounds (excluding 1(2)(e)) without application to a justice, although S.28(4) requires them to investigate the case as soon as practicable and either release the child or remove it to a place of safety as appropriate.

5   In practice, it is usual for the SSD, NSPCC or police to apply for Place of Safety orders because this action is so closely related to any subsequent care proceedings. Furthermore, of the 3 agencies mentioned only the SSD has a range of care facilities and can either receive children into or have them committed to its care.

6   As well as securing the child's immediate safety, the Place of Safety Order provides a breathing space in which the assessment leading to the execution of such an order can be pursued in greater depth, further evidence can be sought and a case prepared, if warranted, for care proceedings.

Care proceedings

7   Section 1 of the 1969 Act states:

"1—(1) Any local authority, constable or authorised person who reasonably believes that there are grounds for making an order under this section in respect of a child or young person may, subject to section 2(3) and (8) of this Act, bring him before a juvenile court.

(2) If the court before which a child or young person is brought under this section is of opinion that any of the following conditions is satisfied with respect to him, that is to say—

(a) his proper development is being avoidably prevented or neglected or his health is being avoidably impaired or neglected or he is being ill-treated; or

(b) it is probable that the condition set out in the preceding paragraph will be satisfied in his case, having regard to the fact that the court or another court has found that that condition is or was satisfied in the case of another child or young person who is or was a member of the household to which he belongs; or

(c) he is exposed to moral danger; or

(d) he is beyond the control of his parent or guardian; or

*(e) he is of compulsory school age within the meaning of the Education Act 1944 and is not receiving efficient full-time education suitable to his age, ability and aptitude; or

*(f) he is guilty of an offence, excluding homicide,

and also that he is in need of care or control which he is unlikely to receive unless the court makes an order under this section in respect of him, then, subject to the following provisions of this section and sections 2 and 3 of this Act, the court may if it thinks fit make such an order.''

An additional condition was inserted after section 1(2)(b) by the Children Act 1975, 3rd Schedule, para 67:

"1—2(bb) it is probable that the conditions set out in paragraph (a) of this subsection will be satisfied in his case, having regard to the fact that a person who has been convicted of an offence mentioned in Schedule 1 to the Act of 1933 is, or may become, a member of the same household as the child.''

The NSPCC is an "authorised person'' under section 1(1).

8 The Home Office "Guide for courts and practitioners'' to Part 1 of the 1969 Act notes in para 14 – 15 that a court can only make a care order where it decides that each of two distinct conditions has been satisfied: first, one of the so-called "primary conditions'' in paragraphs (a) – (f), indicating lack of care or control, and second, the condition at the end of subsection (2), that the child is in need of care or control which he is unlikely to receive unless such an order is made.

9 Medical opinion and evidence, as well as treatment, will be necessary in many but not all cases, and anyone with knowledge of, or contact with, the family is a potential source of evidence. To establish that the child's need for care or control is unlikely to be met unless an order is made, evidence of the family's ability or otherwise to meet these needs and a professional opinion from social workers or others with knowledge of the family may be needed. It is not possible or appropriate in this context to go into the rules of evidence and the standards of proof required in civil (ie care) proceedings as opposed to criminal proceedings. Legal advice in these and other matters is often required and is available to SSDs through the local authority's legal department. The officers of the NSPCC also have access to advice on legal matters within their own agency.

---

* See footnote to para 2

APPENDIX 4 Legal and Procedural Changes Following Recommendations by Inquiries

1   Maria Colwell

(a) *Separate representation.* The Colwell Committee drew attention to the desirability of an independent social worker's view being available in court proceedings where a local authority is seeking or consenting to a change in status of a child under their care or supervision (227). Sections 64 and 65 of the Children Act 1975 were enacted in response to this recommendation and the Magistrates' Courts (Children and Young Persons) Rules 1970 were amended to make provision for the appointment of, and to prescribe the duties of, guardians ad litem. Section 64 is in force only in so far as it provides for the insertion of S.32A(2) to (5) and to S.32(B) (1) and (3) in the C&YP Act 1969.

(b)   *Foster parents.* The Committee also commented "that the court might have been greatly assisted by the presence of the foster parents but they did not attend the hearing. Although they knew that there was to be a hearing they were not served with notice of it officially—the Magistrates' Courts Rules make no provision for foster parents to be served or for them to be given any status at the hearing" (228).

As a result of this comment Rule 14 of the Magistrates' Courts (Children and Young Persons) Rules 1970 was amended to require a person proposing to bring proceedings to include among the people to whom he is already required to send notice of the proceedings "any foster parent or other person with whom the relevant infant has had his home for a period of not less than 6 weeks, ending not more than 6 months before the date of the application, if the whereabouts of such a person is known to the applicant."

(c)   *Medical examination.* The Committee commented that "we consider Miss Lees was greatly handicapped—particularly at the time of the 'April incident'—by not having the power to take Maria forthwith to a doctor" (235). In consequence of this recommendation Rule 28 of the Magistrates' Courts (Children and Young Persons) Rules 1970 was amended to enable a court to add to a supervision order a requirement that the child or young person subject to the order "shall be medically examined in accordance with arrangements made by the supervisor."

(d) *Supervision Regulations.* The Committee commented that "There remains to be considered the desirability or otherwise of making statutory provision for the timing and regularity of visits under a supervision order and of periodic reviews" (237). "While not presuming to generalise, there would have been considerable advantages in Maria's case, and therefore in similar cases, of applying some of the requirements to be found in the [Boarding Out of Children] Regulations of 1955, suitably amended" (239).

As a result of this recommendation section 11A of the Children and Young Persons Act 1969, which enables the Secretary of State to make regulations with respect to the exercise by local authorities of their functions under supervision orders made in care proceedings, was inserted by paragraph 68 of Schedule 3 to the Children Act 1975. Because of their resource implications, no regulations have yet been made.

(e) *Disclosure of information from DHSS records.* The Committee commented on the scanty information which the social services department had about the man who was shortly to become Maria's step-father (216). They examined three possible sources of information: the police, the doctor and social security records. In relation to the latter, while acknowledging the circumstances which make it necessary to respect confidentiality the Committee added:—

"With all those reservations and difficulties, however, we hope that further consideration will be given to the pursuance of enquiries, especially in relation to criminal and health records in certain cases."

Following discussions with the Department about the possibility of easing the strict rules on confidentialty where children are at risk, Departmental instructions to local office staff were amended so as to prescribe the circumstances in which limited information may be given from social security records.

2 John George Auckland

(a) *Notification of release from prison.* The Auckland Committee recommended that shortly before the release of any prisoner convicted of an offence against a child, whether the release be on licence or not, the Social Services Department of the area in which the prisoner is expected to reside should be notified of the impending release and should be able to obtain enough information to assess any risk to a child which may arise on discharge (79, 251(1)). The Committee also recommended that the general practitioner who is expected to have the charge of the prisoner on discharge should be sent a copy of any substantial medical report on the prisoner which has been obtained while he has been in custody and details of any major events in his medical history (illnesses, courses of treatment, etc).

As a result of this recommendation, discussions took place between the Home Office Prison Service and Divisions in DHSS having an interest in the passing of medical information. Circulars LAC(77)8 and (78)22 were issued setting in train procedures on the lines recommended by the Committee.

(b) *Changes in the law.* The Auckland Committee also said "We have been unable to ascertain why in the 1969 Act, Section 2(2)(d) of the 1963 Act was not re-enacted. That provision made it relevant to consider whether a member of the household and previously in a different household ill-treated a child. As the law now stands, Section 1(2)(b) of the 1969 Act, in our view, only admits consideration of other children ill-treated in the same household as the child presently alleged to be at risk of ill-treatment. In fact, it is our opinion that a serious and urgent attempt should be made to re-define the circumstances which must exist before care proceedings can be taken in language which gives adequate protection to children who may be at risk and is readily intelligible to social workers and magistrates" (123).

The Department issued a circular LAC(75)18 on 25 November 1975 clarifying the meaning of section 1(2)(b) of the Children and Young Persons Act 1969 and in response to representations made by the Association of Directors of Social Services in their document "Comments on the Children Bill", a new section 1(2)(bb) was added to the 1969 Act restoring broadly what had been section 2(2)(d) of the CYPA 1963.

3   Stephen Menheniott

The Menheniott report recommended that "Informal undertakings for the provision of social services in the Isles of Scilly, which may have sufficed for an earlier period, are no longer appropriate, and we suggest that there should be an early review of these arrangements" (7.5).

This was a reference to the fact that whilst the provisions of the Children and Young Persons Act 1969 and the Local Authority Social Services Act 1970 covered the Isles of Scilly, they could not be fully administered by the Council of the Isles of Scilly. This was because references to a "local authority" in both Acts could not include the Council, except by order, and no orders had been made. The Islands had therefore had to make informal arrangements with Cornwall County Council to obtain services they could not provide for themselves.

As a result of the Committee's recommendation orders were made. The Isles of Scilly (Children and Young Persons) Order 1980 (SI 1980/327) modifies the 1969 Act by providing that "local authority" in the Act means, for Scilly, the Council of the Isles of Scilly. Similarly, the Isles of Scilly (Local Authority Social Services) Order 1980 (SI 1980/328) provides that the 1970 Act shall have effect in Scilly as if the Council were a local authority for the purposes of the Act.

The Isles of Scilly (National Assistance) Order 1980 (SI 1980/326) makes the same provision in relation to the National Assistance Act 1948.

Printed in England for Her Majesty's Stationery Office by
Hobbs the Printers of Southampton
(1562) Dd718214 C35 8/82 G380